Introduction:
A Journey with Labib
Madanat

T here is nothing like putting yourself into somebody else's shoes and taking a walk with them and listening as they talk along the way to bring a fresh perspective on a situation – even revelation! This is what happened to me one day in November 2010.

I had asked Labib Madanat, a prominent Arab Christian leader in Israel and the wider Middle East, to take me into the heart of the West Bank. I wanted to see for myself what it is really like for the people living there and why he invests so much of his time working with the Palestinian people who live there, the majority of whom are Muslims.

Labib has lived in Jerusalem all his life. He was born there. His father, originally from Jordan, was a pastor there. Labib knows the ancient cobbled streets like the back of his hand. He speaks Arabic, Hebrew and English effortlessly. He understands the Arab culture as well as the Jewish culture as well as the English culture. He is married to an English lady called Carolyn and his dream is to retire to Tunbridge Wells in the UK!

But for Labib, Tunbridge Wells is not an option; it remains a dream. I first met him in 1998. He was then Director of the Palestinian Bible Society, working harmoniously alongside his Israeli Messianic Jewish counterpart. It was then I realized he did not have a negative attitude towards Jewish people or the State of Israel. Rather, he displayed a desire to "reach" them with the gospel in whatever way he could. Since then his job has increased in scope and today he is co-ordinating the work of teams of Palestinian Christians and Messianic believers for the Bible Society in the Middle East. It is Labib's desire that his team members also have a heart for both peoples. Instilling what is in your heart into the heart of another surely comes from example. I have met a number of people, both Jews and Arabs, who work closely with Labib. It is clear that he has inspired them to have hearts that desire forgiveness and reconciliation.

I remember him telling me of one occasion when two of his brothers and colleagues (Arab/Palestinian Christians) were being held at a checkpoint between Israel and the West Bank. They had been told to sit and wait in their car whilst their passports were being checked. It was a hot day and the hours passed. Most people would find this frustrating and infuriating. But these men spent their time praying for the Israeli soldiers who were delaying their journey.

When eventually a soldier did return their passports and allow them to proceed, they asked if they could pray for him and his sick relative.

The soldier looked surprised. "How did you know I have a sick relative?" he asked.

"Because we have been praying for you and God has shown us that your mother is seriously ill."

Meet Me at the Olive Tree

MEET ME AT THE OLIVE TREE

Stories of Jews and Arabs
reconciled to the Messiah

Julia Fisher

MONARCH
BOOKS

Oxford, UK & Grand Rapids, Michigan, USA

Published by Monarch Books
an imprint of
Lion Hudson plc
Wilkinson House, Jordan Hill Road,
Oxford OX2 8DR, England
Email: monarch@lionhudson.com
www.lionhudson.com/monarch

ISBN 978 0 85721 228 3
e-ISBN 978 0 85721 404 1

First edition 2012

Acknowledgments
Scripture quotations taken from the Holy Bible, New International Version, copyright © 1973, 1978, 1984 International Bible Society. Used by permission of Hodder & Stoughton, a member of the Hodder Headline Group. All rights reserved. "NIV" is a trademark of International Bible Society. UK trademark number 1448790.

A catalogue record for this book is available from the British Library

Printed and bound in the UK, February 2014, LH26.

*This book is dedicated to our
grandchildren, that they may grow
up to understand God's mysterious
plan of salvation for all mankind
and carry His heart for the believers
living in Israel and the wider
Middle East at this time.*

By the same author

Israel, the Mystery of Peace (True Potential Publishing)
Future for Israel (True Potential Publishing)
Israel's New Disciples (Monarch)

Contents

Map of the Holy Land   8

Acknowledgments   9

Introduction: A journey with Labib Madanat   11

1	Oded Cohen	21
2	Thomas Damianos	33
3	Zak Mishriky	41
4	Ron Cantor	49
5	Maron and Angelika Raheb	59
6	Peter and Yarden Nasser	71
7	Joshua Pex	83
8	Simon Azazian	91
9	Yoyakim Figueras	103
10	"C", an Arab Christian	113
11	Etti Shoshani	123
12	Sabha Asmar	131
13	Dan and Dalia Alon	139
14	Azar Ajaj and NETS	151
15	Ofer Amitai	163

Postscript: The Story of the Olive Tree Reconciliation Fund

179

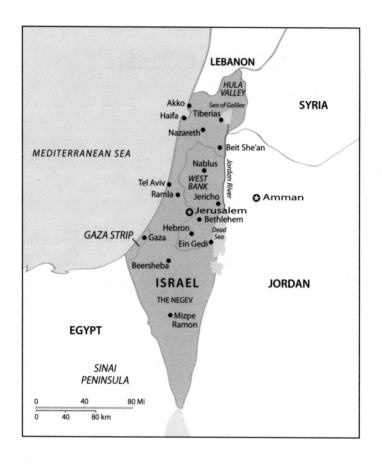

LEBANON

SYRIA

HULA VALLEY

Akko

Sea of Galilee

Haifa

Tiberias

Nazareth

Beit She'an

MEDITERRANEAN SEA

Nablus

WEST BANK

Jordan River

Tel Aviv

Ramla

Jericho

Amman

Jerusalem

Bethlehem

Hebron

GAZA STRIP

Gaza

Dead Sea

Ein Gedi

Beersheba

ISRAEL

JORDAN

THE NEGEV

EGYPT

Mizpe Ramon

SINAI PENINSULA

0   40   80 Mi

0   40   80 km

Acknowledgments

No book is published without the support and encouragement of the publisher. In this case, my grateful thanks go to Tony Collins who, once again, has shown his belief in the importance of the stories contained between the covers of this book.

A book of true stories depends entirely on the co-operation of the people featured. It is a brave decision to allow somebody else to write your story, especially when that story is costly. So, I would like to acknowledge everybody who has willingly allowed their story to be included in this book in order that you, the reader, can enter their world to gain some insight into what God is doing in Israel and the wider Middle East at this time in world history.

The Jewish soldier put down his gun and started weeping as the Palestinians prayed for his family, and then they continued on their journey.

It's not often you hear stories like that, but Labib will tell you that as a Palestinian living in Israel, travelling through Ben Gurion Airport – something he does regularly – is a personal nightmare for him. Without fail he is stopped and searched. What is his response? "Ben Gurion is my mission field," he says with a smile on his face. "When I tell them that I am a Palestinian Arab Christian, and that I love the God of Israel and their Messiah, I get their full attention!"

Labib believes we are living in strategic times and that it won't be too long before Israel realizes who her Messiah is and rushes to embrace Him. As an Arab Christian he realizes he has a part to play in this transformation and part of that job is working amongst the Muslim Palestinian people.

I regularly visit Bethlehem and Jericho in the West Bank. I've visited Ramallah and Bir Zeit. But on this occasion I wanted to go beyond those places to meet the people living in a town or village that few Western Christians had visited. I had heard about the growing number of Muslim Background Believers (MBBs) – secret believers living in fear of losing their lives, not to mention their jobs (if they have one). I wanted to know how many Palestinians living in the West Bank get to hear the true story about Jesus.

The current upheaval in the Arab world has highlighted once again the unbridled hatred that many Muslims have towards Israel – especially those Muslims whom we, in the West, have come to call "radicalized extremists". However, although this may be true, when talking to Labib, who understands better than I the way an Arab would look at the same situation, a different viewpoint emerges that reveals that the hatred is not just one way.

"The hatred is mutual," he says, "although expressed differently and in a more restrained manner among extreme Jewish terrorists, because of the rule of law in Israel and the general trust among Jewish Israelis that their government and the Israeli army deal with the Palestinian Muslim Arab issues. In the Arab world, people do not trust that their governments are dealing with the issues of the Israeli Jewish occupation (or America, for that matter). That is why they express themselves through acts of terror, extreme and harsh words, demonstrations and the burning of flags."

Watching the news unravel on our television screens could cause us to wonder just where these events are leading.

On the other hand, the Bible indicates that sometime in the future, "all Israel will be saved" (Romans 11:26) and that Jewish people will be made "envious" by Gentile believers in Jesus (11:11). So who are these Gentile Christians?

I arranged to meet Labib at the American Colony Hotel in East Jerusalem at nine in the morning. After drinking mint tea and discussing the plan for the day, we set off for Jericho, where he wanted to briefly visit some of his team to encourage them. Then we proceeded to drive up the Jordan Valley before turning left into the central area of the West Bank.

The first thing that struck me was how beautiful it was. Of course, we were driving through the hills of Samaria! And today, many of those hillsides (which are very high in places) are covered in olive trees. From time to time we passed through a small village. There were few cars on the road. We saw very few people. There is a lot of empty space here – a lot of unoccupied land that, Labib told me, "has been owned by Palestinian families for many generations". Most of the houses were humble, simple dwellings whilst others were large and elaborate. The majority of the people we passed looked poor. We saw children playing in the streets. We saw donkeys being ridden whilst others were being led, laden with goods; some of them looked like moving bushes.

We were heading for a town called X (it would not be wise of me to name it).

Labib told me, "I'm going to take you to meet M" (I have disguised the identity of this man for reasons of personal safety), "a Christian Arab who has been working alone amongst the people of this small town for seven years. The town is entirely Muslim. There is a great deal of need and M has been helping them in any way he can."

As we drove along I was full of questions. When were these villages built? How many people live in the West Bank? How many have jobs? Where do they work? Do all the children go to school? Are they free to travel from village to village? Patiently and thoughtfully, Labib answered every question in a calm and restrained manner, careful in his use of language.

The deeper we drove into the hills of Samaria, which today is known as the West Bank, the more I became aware of "settlements" on the tops of the hills. These were Jewish communities. There are some words that immediately provoke an angry, negative reaction, and "settlements" is one of those words. I have noticed that in many people's understanding, "settlements" has come to define Jewish people who have snatched land from the Palestinians in order to build entirely Jewish neighbourhoods. Is this true?

"Not always, but many times," Labib replied.

As we approached X, it appeared that in the case of this village, it was true. "The Palestinians used to live on the top of that hill where there are now Jewish people living," Labib explained, "and the Palestinians were forced to leave their homes and subsequently built a new town lower down the hillside. As a result the Palestinian villagers lost their farmland and access to roads."

I was trying to put myself in their shoes and could understand that the Palestinians living in X had a low opinion of the Jewish people who had "occupied" their homes and taken their land. Here were two peoples living side by side, watching each other suspiciously, hating each other, distrusting each other, but never actually meeting.

I met M at a community centre in X. He was friendly, and delighted to see Labib. As they exchanged greetings and news I took the opportunity to look around. There were a number of women and young children in the centre. I noticed the walls had been painted with pictures displaying natural beauty – birds, trees, children playing. Weaving through the pictures were words in Arabic – to my untrained eye it looked like poetry. I later found out they were words from the Bible:

> *Love is patient, love is kind. It does not envy, it does not boast, it is not proud. It is not rude, it is not self-seeking, it is not easily angered, it keeps no record of wrongs. Love does not delight in evil but rejoices with the truth. It always protects, always trusts, always hopes, always perseveres. Love never fails.*
> *1 Corinthians 13:4–8*

M was happy to tell me about the centre and explained how it was used to help local "marginalized people" and provide a meeting-place, especially for women, children and the youth. He explained that today, the local government of X, which is under the jurisdiction of the Palestinian Authority, covers several villages in the West Bank, and the entire area is Muslim.

"I became a Christian in the Alliance Church in the Old City of Jerusalem," he told me, "and experienced the love of Jesus, which changed my perspective on life. We need to bring the love of Jesus to the people to help them live in this hard situation. We need to reflect His love and compassion and mercy, and encourage them and tell them, 'It's OK – there is occupation, but still there is hope, and if you focus on this hope you will be strong and you will not be for ever in this hard situation.' So we are trying to bring hope to the people. I tell them not to focus on the enemy and how to fight them. Rather, I tell them God will bring justice to the people – give Him the chance to work.

"I tell them about the verses in the Bible that talk about love… they are shocked and blessed! I explain what is meant by patience, especially when you are in a difficult situation. We started designing a programme about love and the language of love as a tool of communication. They have no hope in life and are empty, but if we keep talking about the love of God for them, they will have hope in this bad situation.

"After six or seven years of working here, I feel part of this community and they are not angry when I talk to them; they trust me and they see the love that I have and the energy I have to help them and their children. I am not here to

17

convert people; rather, I am here to serve. It is important that we are humble.

"Looking forward, my vision is to see reconciliation between Palestinians and Jews. I long to organize activities between the Jews who live in the old town of X – the people who stole the land – and the Palestinians here. I long for them to understand that it is not just about land. It's hard to forget, but I pray that people will come to the point where they don't want borders, but rather want to share a meal with each other. I believe it can happen, but we need the grace of God to fill this area."

I also met a young woman who works with M in the community centre. Let's call her J. She told me about her life – and it was hard. Her dream was to go and live in Dubai where she believed she would enjoy a better standard of living. I asked her what she thought of Jewish people. Looking me straight in the eye, she told me she had hated all Jews. That was until just a few months ago, during the long hot summer, when she witnessed a simple act of human kindness that was to change her worldview.

J had been queuing at a checkpoint to cross into another area. She had been stood waiting for over two hours and the temperature was soaring. Just in front of her was a mother with a young child, who was becoming distressed by the heat and thirst. All of a sudden a Jewish soldier walked up to this mother and offered her and her child a drink of water. "This was the first time I had ever seen a Jewish person being kind to a Palestinian, and it melted my heart," she told me. "I now know it's possible for us to live in peace, because they have hearts just like us."

That such a simple act of kindness could change a

person's outlook on life was very moving. On the drive back to Jerusalem, I discussed this story with Labib. He, like M, understands how important it is to encourage individuals, because it only takes one person to make a difference to another person's life, and that in turn can affect many others when the story is shared.

"What keeps you here?" I asked him, "when you could be enjoying a much easier life in America or Tunbridge Wells?"

"If I didn't believe that it's the job of us Arab Christians to provoke the Jews to envy, I'd be out of here tomorrow," he replied. "Who is most capable of making the Jewish people jealous? It's us! It's a family dispute that we are experiencing here in the Middle East. Jealousy in a family runs deep. This dispute has gone on for generations. But the Apostle Paul makes it clear in his letter to the Romans that 'all Israel will be saved' [Romans 11:26]. He also says, 'Did God's people stumble and fall beyond recovery? Of course not! His purpose was to make his salvation available to the Gentiles, and then the Jews would be jealous and want it for themselves'" [Romans 11:11, paraphrase].

As we approached Jerusalem, I had one more question for Labib. Does he really believe that Palestinians living in the West Bank in an entirely Muslim culture will one day respond to the gospel and believe in Jesus as the Son of God and embrace their Jewish neighbours?

"They already are, and that is what keeps me here," he replied without hesitation.

Perhaps this true story demonstrates the depth of what God is doing in Israel and the Palestinian Areas today. Maybe, because God works in such mysterious ways, it is easy to miss what is going on in the spiritual realm; our attention is so often drawn to the secular media's attention on the "conflict". The recent upheavals in the Arab nations of the world are an example of this.

This book (which is based on a series of radio programmes called *The Olive Tree*) is written to bring the stories of what God is doing in the Middle East to our attention. If Jesus is the Messiah, then it is no wonder that both Orthodox Jews and Muslims are disturbed by this and feel threatened, and therefore often react aggressively. In the following pages you will read the stories of former Orthodox Jews who are now believers in Jesus (or Yeshua). You will read of Palestinian Christians who understand, like Labib, that some time soon Jewish people living in Israel will recognize their Messiah and that it is their job to help them find Him. They also know that it is their job to share the gospel message with their own people, the Muslim majority.

By the time you reach the end of the book I believe you will find that your mind has been stretched and your heart thrilled as you too embrace all that God is doing through both Jewish believers and Arab/Palestinian Christians living in Israel and the wider Middle East in these days.

Julia Fisher
January 2012

Chapter 1
Oded Cohen

oday Oded Cohen and his wife Bimini are missionaries with *Jews for Jesus* in Israel – something he never would have imagined!

One of the fascinating things about meeting believers in Israel is that each person has an interesting story to tell about how they came to believe that Jesus/Yeshua is actually the Messiah of Israel. Often these stories are funny. Invariably they involve a struggle. And often they are costly.

I first met Oded at the *Jews for Jesus* offices in Tel Aviv to record a radio interview with him for *The Olive Tree* series. It soon became clear that his story could not be contained in a thirteen-minute interview, so I sat back and let him talk. Like most Israelis, he has a dry sense of humour, he does not take himself too seriously and is extremely unpretentious.

To be a missionary with *Jews for Jesus* in Israel takes some courage, and for Oded it has been a long journey. His story begins on a kibbutz in southern Israel where he was born. Whilst a few kibbutzim are home to religious Jewish people and adhere to strict religious laws, the kibbutz where Oded grew up, like most of the kibbutzim in

Israel, was entirely secular. There, the subject of God was either ignored or avoided. Instead, the emphasis was on building the physical State of Israel, reclaiming the land and defending the country.

Oded takes up the story.

I grew up believing that if there is a God, He is far away and has nothing to do with us. Not only did I not believe in God, I and everyone else from our kibbutz were fiercely anti-God. There was, and still is, a power struggle between the religious and secular Jews in Israel, so we grew up resenting the religious people. We served in the army and they did not. Whilst we were spending some of the best years of our lives running and sweating and fighting, they were sitting in a *yeshiva* studying the Torah (the first five books in the Bible, which include the Mosaic laws), or whatever it is they study. We felt that a small minority of religious Jews were trying to dictate to us secular Israelis how to live our lives. We resented that nothing was open on the Sabbath. There was no transportation. No restaurants. No movies. We resented the fact that they took all our fun away and consequently, if that was what God was all about, we wanted nothing to do with it.

When I and all the other children on our kibbutz were growing up, we developed our own tradition on Yom Kippur. This is supposed to be the holiest and most solemn day of the year – a day of fasting and repentance. However, we did not fast; rather, we delighted in preparing a big barbeque feast that filled the entire kibbutz with the aroma of food, and if we could get hold of a pig to roast, that was a double accomplishment for us!

From a very young age we all knew we were the "chosen

people" but we never understood what "chosen" meant. We presumed it meant that we were the best. We were very proud of our achievements. We had the best army in the world and the best agriculture; we were able to make the desert bloom.

After I had served four years in the army I decided, like most Israelis, to travel the world. I briefly stopped in the United States to see my brother before travelling on to South America, where I backpacked around for a year. I then went back to the United States, which was very attractive to me. It felt like I was living the American dream and that I could achieve whatever I wanted to. I could be free to live my life as I chose without anyone dictating to me what I should do. (When I lived on the kibbutz, our entire schedule was structured and set by others.)

I thought, when I left Israel, I would only be away for one year. But once I arrived in the United States I soon realized I could have anything I wanted. I bought a car. On the kibbutz we shared cars and if we wanted to drive anywhere, we had to book a car at least a week in advance and, by the time the day arrived, you probably might have changed your mind! But in America I had my own car and I could go wherever I liked, whenever I wanted. There was such a sense of freedom.

The American dream bug caught me and I decided I wanted to make a lot of money. Little did I know what was going to happen!

After a year of travelling, I met the woman who was to become my wife. Bimini is a Chinese American with a nominal Catholic background. She did not hold to any deep religious faith. During our first four years of marriage, Bimini was exposed to many Jewish traditions, including the celebration of the Jewish holidays. After hearing bits of the

Bible and singing beautiful praise songs to a God we didn't really know, Bimini began to sense that the God of Israel is a personal God who did not just abandon His people, and she decided she would like to convert to Judaism. She began reading the Torah and began looking for a rabbi to teach her how to become Jewish. Whilst I was happy, my parents were elated that I would finally have a "real" Jewish wife!

However, soon after we met a wonderful Christian couple who shared their faith with us and gave us a Bible, complete with the New Testament. At that time, my wife was a little bogged down reading the book of Leviticus. We both really love animals, and she could not understand why all the blood sacrifices were necessary. So she stopped reading the Old Testament and delved right into the Gospel of John. Within a couple of months she came to believe that Jesus is the Jewish Messiah and the Saviour of the world. God healed her broken heart and filled her life with joy and peace.

I was extremely disappointed at this point. What was I going to do?! Not only was she no longer going to become "Jewish", but she had now turned Christian on me! Then she tried to convert me! She told me there was no contradiction between being Jewish and being Christian, because Jesus is the Jewish Messiah. I told her it was all right for her to believe that, but I was Jewish and Jewish people do not believe such things!

One day, whilst walking along a street, Bimini met a man who was wearing a *Jews for Jesus* T-shirt. She explained to him that she needed help in persuading her Jewish husband to believe in Jesus. I eventually agreed to meet him, but in my mind I had decided to challenge him so much that he would leave me alone. Besides, I was convinced that he would be unable to answer my questions.

So a *Jews for Jesus* missionary named David visited us first, but even though I was polite and listened, I was not very interested. Several months later, Garrett, also from *Jews for Jesus*, came to our home to share the gospel with me. I told him that I wanted him to show me from my Bible [i.e. the Old Testament], and not from the New Testament, where it says that Jesus is the Jewish Messiah. And, to my surprise, he took me through all the Messianic prophecies in the Hebrew Bible and showed me how Jesus had fulfilled them, one by one. I was shocked because I had never seen this before. I had studied the Bible in Israel as a child, but nobody had ever mentioned those prophecies – and certainly nobody had ever mentioned Jesus. Although it started to make some sense in my head, I still believed that I could not be Jewish and believe in Jesus. After several meetings with Garrett, he finally told me that there was nothing more he could show me for now, and it was time for me to ask the God I knew of – the God of Abraham, Isaac and Jacob – to reveal Himself to me and to show me who Jesus is. I dismissed his suggestion. How could anybody talk to God like that (if God even existed)? But I told him I would give it a try.

It was then that some amazing things began to happen. My wife and I cared for a number of pet rabbits in our home – animals that we had rescued – and one of them, named Chloe, was paralysed in both back legs. We had taken this poor rabbit to the best veterinarian. We also took her for various treatments, such as acupuncture and acupressure, physical therapy, and a chiropractor. You name it, we tried it! In California there are a lot of alternative medicines available. We had spent so much money on this poor rabbit, but nothing had helped. One day, while feeling sorry for her, I stroked her head as she sat on my lap. I thought to myself, "Wait! Let's see what 'He' can do about it." So I closed my eyes and laid my hand on the rabbit's head and said, "Jesus, if you are who they say you are, let's see you heal this rabbit." Before I had even opened my eyes, the rabbit jumped off my lap and hopped on all four legs around and around the room before coming back to me. I was stunned. But after the initial shock had worn off I said to myself, "Wow! That sure was some coincidence!" I didn't want to believe that God had answered my prayer; I was so stubborn.

Of course, I didn't tell my wife about this. I didn't want her to be right! Time and time again, over a long period of time, I continued to test God, and He kept on answering.

At that time, for about three years, I had been suffering from a painful inflammation of the hip. If I sat for too long, I would experience severe pain in one hip when I got up and walked. One day, whilst driving to work, I thought, "Let's see what 'He' can do about that." And again I said, "Jesus, if you are who they say you are, let's see if you can take care of that pain." I totally forgot about it and after about a week I caught myself thinking, "When was the last time I felt that pain in my hip?" It was completely gone, and to this day it hasn't come back. But once again, I persuaded myself that maybe my hip had gotten better by itself. Maybe something in my diet or in my exercise regime had helped. (Never mind that I had no special diet and no exercise regime!)

Also during this time, I was having many dreams. I remember in one of my dreams I saw a big healthy tree with a thick trunk, but it had been felled at the point where the branches started. At the foot of the trunk, close to the ground, a healthy branch was growing that was covered in leaves. I woke up in the morning remembering this vivid picture. As I thought about it, I wondered whether the big tree was Judaism and the branch growing out of it was Christianity – and maybe Judaism and Christianity were not contradictions after all, but rather a continuation sharing the same root. This time I shared the dream with my wife. I had never seen that picture anywhere else before. Bimini explained to me that the Bible uses the same description. She took me to the book of Romans and I read how Christians, the wild olive shoot, are grafted into the cultivated olive tree, the people of Israel.

By this time my wife had become a "full-blown" Christian. She would spend hours every week out on the streets sharing her faith with strangers. I criticized her for that. "How phoney can you be?" I would say. "You meet somebody on the street that you have never met before and you tell them that Jesus loves them. How do you know that Jesus loves them? You could be talking to a criminal!" Bimini explained to me that she did it out of obedience to the teaching of Jesus, who commanded His believers to love everybody, in the same way that He loves everybody, and because she didn't want anyone to be condemned to hell. I have to admit, I didn't really buy this obedience idea. Neither did I believe that God would judge anyone.

That night, I dreamt again and in my dream I saw my favourite radio show host, Geoff Metcalf. I had such a high regard for this man, I believed everything he said. In my dream he told me to read the story of Lot's wife. I woke up in the morning and I had no idea what the story of Lot's wife was all about. So I asked my wife, "What is the story of Lot's wife all about?"

She realized something had happened in the night. She asked me, "Oded, who told you to read the story of Lot's wife?" When I told her it was Geoff Metcalf, she laughed. "Oded, that wasn't Geoff Metcalf, that was God; but you wouldn't take it from God, so He disguised Himself as Geoff Metcalf so you would listen to Him!"

When I read the story, it made perfect sense because it was about obedience and disobedience.

After about a year and a half of testing God and denying the miracles, something happened that finally made me believe in Jesus. I came home from work one day feeling very feverish and I knew I would be in bed for a few days recovering. I was so weak and miserable that I was willing to do anything to feel better. So, for the first time, instead of testing God, I just threw myself on the bed and opened my arms and said, "Jesus, I open my heart to you. I need help – please heal me." I fell asleep like a baby.

The next morning I woke up feeling like a totally new person. Not only was I completely healed, but I knew I had received a brand-new heart. I raised my hands and said, "God, I give up, I surrender."

I thought to myself, "How many signs? How many miracles? How many dreams? How blind must you be before you realize that God is trying to show you something?"

And my life has never been the same since.

During the next three years I joined my wife in volunteering with *Jews for Jesus*. We would help in any way we could, often behind the scenes. Then one day David Brickner, the Executive Director of *Jews for Jesus*, invited us to his office to talk about the ministry and asked if we would prayerfully consider joining them. My dream about becoming rich and lazy was still strong in my mind and I knew that if we joined the ministry that would be the end of my dream! So I agreed that we would pray about it.

At the back of my mind I also knew that if I joined the ministry it would be very hard for my parents to accept; aside from their son believing in Jesus, it would be a shameful admission to have a son as a missionary. God forbid! I wanted to be able to visit my parents on a regular basis and maintain a close relationship with them. If I joined the ministry, I knew I would no longer have that freedom because my parents would be ashamed and embarrassed about what I was doing.

At this same time Bimini and I were enrolled in a Bible study course and we were studying the book of Matthew. I remember there were two lessons that really spoke to me. The first was the story of the rich young ruler. As I was driving the forty-minute journey home, I asked myself what was standing between me and God; what would be hard for me to give up in order to follow Jesus? At the same time I was wondering why God had saved me and what His purpose was for my life. Another question I had was, "Can I really say I have made Jesus the Lord of my life?" I still had my own plans and desires, and in all honesty I couldn't say that. So whilst driving along I strongly heard God telling me, "Oded, forget about being rich. Forget about being able to do whatever you want. Come and work for me and I'll provide all you need."

There was one further problem that stood in my way – another rabbit! When I left Israel the hardest thing for me to leave was my dog. How do you explain to an animal that you will be back sometime in the future? It was then I promised myself that if I had another animal, I would commit to looking after it for its entire life. In addition, this rabbit was ill, and it was hard for me to just abandon her and break that commitment. So I asked God, "But what about Penelope?" – that was her name! As soon as I had asked that question, I felt that all communication with God was cut off. I understood that God was saying to me that I was not meant to question Him; if God had said He would provide all our needs, He meant it. A few days later Penelope passed peacefully away. Now, we had rescued many pet rabbits and Penelope had been ill for a long time. But I knew this rabbit's death was unique and that it was connected with that communication with God. I sensed that God had taken her.

During another Bible study class we were studying the implication of the words of Jesus when He said, "Pick up your cross and follow me." Again I had the same question: "Can I really pick up the cross and follow Him? Can I let go of everything I want to do and follow Jesus?"

It became clear to me that was what I needed to do. I told my wife (who had been quite sure for some time that we were being called to serve with *Jews for Jesus*) that it was time for us to go back and see David Brickner and agree to work for the organization.

That was ten years ago now.

So, you ask, what does it mean to be back in Israel with my Chinese-American wife, working as missionaries taking the gospel to the towns and villages within Israel? It means a lot. Firstly, the fact that I have returned to live in Israel surprises me. It wasn't my plan. We were comfortable in America and we had no reason to come back here, where life is much harder. When you get used to the United States it makes no sense to live here. But four years ago, during one of our visits to Israel, we were sitting in a café in Jerusalem when we both sensed the same call and turned to each other and realized it was time to come and share with God's people in Israel.

However, there was an immediate problem because my wife didn't speak Hebrew. In addition, she was not used to Israeli culture or Israeli food. How would she be able to minister to people in Israel?

For me it was very clear. When God says "Go", you go. When God sent Abraham, he didn't say, "But what will Sarah do?" However, whilst it was clear to me, I did not want to force my wife to do anything against her will. So we came for a short while and helped with one of the *Jews for Jesus* campaigns in Israel, and it soon became clear that she would have no problem.

Now that we are here, it is amazing to see what God is doing in the land. As we work on the campaigns we are seeing so much openness and curiosity. There is a lot of opposition as well, but we expect that!

As I look forward to the next few years, I am expecting to see a great revival in Israel. When that will be I don't know. In the meantime I just want to remain faithful to His calling.

As for my parents, they have come a long way in their thinking. Recently they even came with us to a Messianic congregation. They would probably prefer it if I was doing something different, but they have accepted my decision to be a believer in Jesus and are far more open now to what we are doing. I see the same change in Israelis; whereas a few years ago people would not have been prepared to talk about

Jesus, today that has all changed and many people now know someone who is a believer. There are many congregations now all over Israel. So it is a most exciting time to be here in Israel and it is a wonderful privilege to be a part of all that God is doing.

Chapter 2
Thomas Damianos

T homas Damianos was born in Haifa to a Greek father and an Arab mother. As a child he was brought up in the Greek Orthodox Church. He went on to study at the Technion – the Israel Institute of Technology in Haifa – where he qualified first as an architect. He then studied civil engineering and worked in that field for fifteen years. He then studied law and today he is a practising lawyer.

However, Thomas' life has been shaped more by his faith than his professions. His story is unique and the work he is now doing to bring Arab Christian students together with Messianic Jewish students is the realization of a dream he had a few years ago. He believes the future of Israel depends on believers in Jesus being united – Jew and Arab – and he has found a way of bringing about that unity. To achieve this dream involved Thomas in further study – this time of the Bible, and at the time of writing he is just finishing a post-graduate degree.

What drives Thomas to work so hard? It is quite simply his passion to draw Jewish and Arab students together to study the Bible in order to develop a group of like-minded believers in Jesus who can demonstrate to Israeli Jews and Arabs that in Jesus, unity is possible; all this in a land under constant pressure from attack, both from within and from without.

Thomas' story reveals how one man, with an unshakeable belief in the vision God has put into his heart, can change the attitudes of many others who, in turn, can change the opinion of many more.

When I met Thomas in Netanya to record his story, the thing that struck me about him was the sheer joy with which he spoke about his life and how one thing had led to another. He picks up the story now.

Our family was Greek Orthodox. Sixty years ago, when living in Israel, my grandfather became a believer.

My journey of faith began twelve years ago when my brother Carlos became a believer. It was amazing. He was younger than me but I watched from a distance how dramatically his life changed, but at that time I didn't know who or what had affected my brother in such a favourable way. It was a few years before I heard the full story. As we were talking, I asked him what had happened to make him such a different person, and it was then that he told me about Jesus. I told him that I knew about Jesus and read the Bible often. But there was something more about the Jesus he talked about – and I had to admit that I had never "met" Him!

Eventually we prayed together and I became a believer and started going to the Emmanuel Evangelical Church in Haifa, and I am still there today. The pastor there, Najeeb Atteih, is my cousin, and it's great because I know what his life was like before he became a Christian. It's amazing, and now we are serving the Lord together and I am an elder of the church.

Fifteen years ago I completed my degrees in architecture and civil engineering at the Technion in Haifa. After fifteen years working as a civil engineer, I studied for a BA in Bible Studies and another BA in Religious Studies (comparative religion), which was very interesting. I am now finishing my Master's Degree in Bible Studies. Two years ago I began to teach the Bible and currently I am teaching students at the Israel College of the Bible. Also, four months ago I finished my Law degree (LLB) and I am practising as a lawyer now.

So today I am earning my living as a lawyer and at the same time I am a Bible teacher at the church and at the college. This is the fulfilment of a dream I had five years ago.

Now, I love Arabs because I am an Arab! But I also love Jews because I have a lot of Jewish friends. Haifa, where I live, is a unique place. Arabs and Jews live happily together in this city. For some years I was thinking about what I could do to encourage Arabs and Jews to mix together more. I thought that using the gift God gave me to teach the Bible was the place to start. So I began a class to teach the Bible through a programme of Theological Education by extension to Arabs. But my dream was to teach Arabs and Jews together.

Two years ago I had a meeting with the President of the Israel College of the Bible, Dr Erez Soref, and I shared with him my vision. And it was amazing, because although the college is primarily for Messianic Jewish believers, he told me that was his vision also! As we talked, we agreed that if we began classes for potential leaders from both Arab churches and Jewish congregations, we could gradually change the political and spiritual climate in Israel over the next ten, twenty or thirty years. By studying together, these people would have an opportunity to really get to know each other. They would be able to discuss deep matters and find that through their common faith in Jesus they would become "one", because Jesus unites people and makes us "one". We agreed that as they finished their degrees and became elders and leaders in their churches and congregations, they would be in a strong position to change the mindset of the people by teaching them from the Bible how we can be one and together demonstrate to our fellow Israelis that both unity and peaceful co-existence are possible.

The Israel College of the Bible's website states that it is a "Messianic educational institution that exists to equip and develop leaders in Messiah's service and to provide a unique understanding of the Jewish roots of our faith. Our emphasis and the majority of our programmes are focused on training Israelis, but we believe that as Jewish believers we should also be a light to the nations."

So it is clear that the meeting Thomas had with Dr Erez Soref, the Jewish President of the ICB, was a watershed moment in the life of the college. Thomas describes how the new programme began:

In 2010 we began the programme at the Israel College of the Bible – a Messianic Jewish college – and it was amazing. For the first time at the college, we celebrated Christmas! Ten Arab students joined the course and from the start they wanted to help the Jewish students know about the meaning behind our Christian holidays. They decided to begin with Christmas and they shared with their Jewish counterparts the true meaning of Christmas. At the same time, the Jewish students introduced the Arab students to the biblical feasts and we joined with them at Pessach (the feast of Passover) and Succot (the feast of Tabernacles).

And so it was that on 23 December 2010, the Israel College of the Bible celebrated Christmas on its new campus, with all the students participating – Arab, Jewish and internationals, as well as staff, faculty and the worship team.

The celebration began as ICB President Dr Erez Soref greeted all participants, and prayed in Hebrew, followed by prayers in Arabic by Pastor Ihab Ashkar, and in English by Professor Larry Goldberg. The worship team sang Christmas songs in three languages – Arabic, Hebrew and English. Thomas Damianos then spoke about the significance of Christmas to Jews, Arabs and all nations, and explained the holiday's symbols and the meaning of Christmas for Christians worldwide.

The main speech was by Thomas' brother Carlos Damianos, who is an evangelist and an ICB graduate. "Not just a child, but a Saviour is born," he said as he explained the significance of the incarnation that fulfilled the biblical prophecies and through which we are all saved.

The arrival of Santa Claus caused great excitement and he gave gifts to all! Before everybody sat down to enjoy a special festive meal, Thomas Damianos prayed and wished all participants "a Merry Christmas and a Happy New Year".

The degree course takes four years to complete, so I asked Thomas whether, after such a successful start, it has been easy to maintain the enthusiasm and encourage more students to join.

When I tell the Arab students about this idea, they love it. They want to study and have a good relationship with Jews. In Israel we have many difficult political issues which we cannot ignore. In addition, we come from such different cultures and backgrounds. But through our common faith in Jesus we can talk about these issues through His eyes, because we know that there is no difference between Gentiles and Jews, because all of us need Jesus and in Jesus we can be one. When Arab Christians and Jewish believers work together and serve the Lord together, it is a good model for other Israelis – both Jews and Arabs. In the Israel College of the Bible we are experiencing that this works – we can do it. We can feel the love between us. We can pray together.

Looking ahead a few years, I think the effect will be considerable. Already, in our congregation in Emmanuel Church in Haifa, we invite Jewish students to come and speak to the Arab people – and they come! And we go to their Jewish congregations. We share the Bible together. Two or three times a year a number of local Messianic congregations and Arab churches in Haifa meet together. So I think in a few years' time, when the students that are studying now have finished their degrees and are leaders in their congregations, they will know how to bring Arab Christians and Jewish believers together. I know they will do that because this has become their vision also. Their desire is to see mixed Arab and Jewish congregations. We don't have to be separate any longer. We can share the Bible together. We can evangelize together.

My family has become an example of how it is possible to have good relationships between Arab Christians and Jewish Messianic believers. My mother and sister go to a Messianic

Jewish congregation – and they are Arabs! My brother Carlos has married a Messianic Jew! And they have a baby daughter called Christina! They have a great life together and serve the Lord together. Carlos has a special gift from the Lord because he loves not only Jewish people but also Muslims. He is an evangelist not just here in Israel but in other countries too.

Chapter 3
Zak Mishriky

Zak Mishriky is a Palestinian Christian. He was once a member of the Palestinian Liberation Organization (PLO) under Yasser Arafat. Memories of his early life are painful. He started life in a refugee camp. His father was sent to prison. He hated Israelis and resented the State of Israel. Zak was deeply scarred by these experiences. However, today, as well as running a shop in the Old City, he is an evangelist sharing his faith with both Palestinians and Jewish people.

If you have been to Jerusalem and wandered through the streets of the Old City, it is likely you have passed Zak's shop in the Christian Quarter.

To explore the Old City of Jerusalem is a unique experience. With a history that stretches back more than 3,000 years, there is nowhere else quite like it on earth. The Old City is divided culturally and historically into four Quarters: the Jewish Quarter, the Armenian Quarter, the Christian Quarter and the Muslim Quarter.

I have walked around the Old City on numerous occasions and am always enthralled by the very real sense of importance and significance that these streets hold. For religious people of any faith – Christian, Muslim or Jew –

41

Jerusalem is sacred. For the more politically minded, the sense of history and the story of human civilization that has been played out here still echoes around the narrow alleyways. It is as though every stone could tell a story; and that story is far from over. Situated at the crossroads of three continents, throughout history Jerusalem has been (and continues to be) one of the most fought over cities in the world, and in the Old City, you can sense the tension.

The story of Zak Mishriky is rooted in the Christian Quarter, where there are approximately forty "Christian holy sites" including, at its heart, the Church of the Holy Sepulchre. Since the birth of the early church, this site, and later the church that was built there (which is also known as the Church of the Resurrection), has been an important pilgrimage destination for Christians. It stands on the site, formerly outside the city walls, that many biblical archaeologists confidently believe encompasses both Golgotha (Calvary), where Jesus was crucified, and the tomb (sepulchre) where he was buried.

Zak's shop, just a short walk away from the Church of the Holy Sepulchre, is in Christian Quarter Road, the Quarter's main shopping thoroughfare. Zak sells antiquities, including coins, pottery and Roman glass. It is a fascinating shop to visit and Zak knows his business. On one shelf sit some ancient icons – he knows the story behind each one of them. He takes out a tray of coins dating back 2,000 years and enthusiastically explains whose head and inscription is on each one.

Zak, now married with two young children, was born in 1978 and has been running his shop (which has been in his family since 1947) since the mid 1990s. That is where we met to record this interview. Whilst customers came in to look around, Zak told me how he manages to find enough time in the day to run a business, spend time with his family and be an evangelist.

Understandably, it was Zak's early life that initially shaped his thinking. So what was it like for him growing up as a Palestinian living in the Old City of Jerusalem?

Well, if you grow up in the Old City as a Palestinian you have strong political views! You live in Israel but you are not an Israeli; you are a Palestinian. But there is nothing to prove you are Palestinian except what your own mind tells you. It is very complicated.

You went through some difficult times?

Of course. I'm a Palestinian living in Israel and you therefore have to face difficult times.

Did you have a lot of hatred in you?

Yes. I grew up in a refugee camp and my experience of Israel was not good. When I was twelve years old my father went to prison. I was beaten up by Israeli soldiers. By the time I was fifteen I was a leader in the Palestinian Liberation Organization (PLO).

What persuaded you to become a Christian?

The love of Christ. Somebody shared with me that Jesus said, "Love your enemies and pray for those who persecute you" (Matthew 5:44). The first time I read it, I thought it meant that Christ cared more for my enemies than He did about me.

But I quickly realized that Jesus cared so much about me and wanted to heal me of all the hatred that was in my life at that time. I understood that if I hate, I am sick; my inner man is sick. After some of my friends shared Christ with me, I gave my life to Him. At first nothing happened. But two days later I saw Christ in a vision and He set me free from hatred, and my life changed.

Today, as well as running his shop, Zak is an evangelist. He wants to share the gospel with as many people as he can, especially his fellow Palestinians, many of whom are Muslims. This is difficult and sensitive work, as Zak explains.

Yes, this is difficult work. Many of my people often have a wrong idea about Christianity and about who Jesus really is. What makes us unique as Christians is, we know God more, because Jesus said, "If you really knew me, you would know my Father as well. From now on, you do know him and have seen him" (John 14:7). So Jesus made the Father known to us. And for us Christians, we have Christ in us, so we know God more. Many people here in Israel think they know God, but they don't know Him like we do, because they don't know Jesus, who is the only one who makes God the Father known to us. So we try to help people to know God better by telling them about Jesus.

Zak is trying to share his faith with people who are in the same situation he was in as a young man – people who are hurting, who are involved in drugs, who are violent, who are in trouble. So how do they respond when they hear Zak's story?

When they hear how the gospel changed my life, it gives them hope. But I also tell them that my life as a Christian is a daily decision to follow Jesus. I explain to them that my life didn't change automatically... I had to make some hard decisions. I help them to understand that their lives can change too, but they have to be willing to leave their old life and habits behind. In the case of Muslim people, this involves breaking with cultural traditions as well as religious traditions, and it is very difficult and dangerous for them.

Zak is married and has a young family, yet every night he is out leading Bible studies in various places in Jerusalem and elsewhere. He has a passion to share his faith. I asked him what he believes God is doing in Israel and the Palestinian Areas in the West Bank at this time.

It feels as though God's hand is heavy over the whole Middle East and He is increasing the pressure. So people are asking questions; they want to know and they want their lives to be changed. Most people are keen to talk and are very interested to know more about Jesus. They know a little and they want to know more.

Can you tell me one or two stories about the people you are meeting and sharing the Bible with at the moment?

One of the men we are meeting lives in the West Bank. He is a policeman in the Palestinian Authority, a member of their Special Forces. Thirty-eight men are in his team and he is the only Christian – the rest are Muslim. When I first met him, he was not a strong believer but he was trying to live a

Christian life. He told me about another man in his team who was always watching him. He would ask, "Why do we have this Christian guy with us? Why is he different?"

When I met this policeman he, like so many Christians there, felt isolated and had no fellowship with others. I told him more about Christ. I explained how He changes our inner life to make us different, so that our principles are different and our point of view is different to those we live amongst. He then faced many difficulties at home and finally his wife left him – she couldn't live with him now that he had become a Christian.

Two weeks ago we were having a Bible study and we prayed for his family. He understood that although his wife had left him, if he wanted her to come back, he had to love her with the love of Christ. God answered our prayers; his attitudes changed and he was able to influence his wife by loving her and bringing her back to the home. Life is difficult for them and they do not have a lot of money. But he realized that what is inside him, what is in his heart, is more important than material possessions. With the right attitude in his heart, he realized he could bring about peace in his marriage.

Zak spends much time meeting with Palestinians, so I asked him if he had the desire and the opportunity to meet with Jewish believers.

I have no problem with Messianic Jews. We have some problems with Israelis, but Messianic believers – no problem! We have lots of good Messianic Jewish friends who support us. We enjoy good fellowship; there are many things that unite us. There is one particular Jewish man, and his young family, that my wife and I are particularly friendly with; we sit together from time to time and talk about various things. We enjoy a barbeque together and we let our kids play together. I do not want my children to grow up and experience the struggles I went through. Rather, our children are brought up to understand the Kingdom of God, where there are Arabs and Jews together. We need to be reminded all the time that we do not belong to this group or that group – rather, we belong to the Lord of Hosts. Our physical body often wants to make a stand and fight, often for high principles, but we always need to remember that Christ has higher principles and that Jesus conquered the whole world without using any weapons. Love and peace are stronger than war and hatred.

If you are in Jerusalem and would like to visit Zak's shop, the address is 24 Christian Quarter Road. Or visit his website, www.oldcityjerusalemgifts.com

Chapter 4
Ron Cantor

T oday Ron Cantor describes himself as a Messianic Jewish Communicator, which means he has travelled a very long way from his roots.

He grew up in Richmond, Virginia in the United States in a traditional Jewish home. He went through the two essential rites of passage for Jewish boys – he was circumcised at eight days old and celebrated his Bar Mitzvah when he was thirteen years old. In addition to his formal schooling, he attended Hebrew school three times a week to study Jewish life and culture until his Bar Mitzvah.

He was raised believing that Jesus was not the Messiah. Ron admits he was not religious, but neither was he an atheist; he just did not see any clear evidence for God. What really interested the young Ron Cantor was having fun.

His destiny in life could have been very different, but when he was seventeen a schoolfriend called Brian started to influence Ron's thinking, because Brian became a believer in Jesus. Seeing this change in his friend unsettled the fun-loving Ron Cantor, and he started asking some deep questions about life and death. He began to think about God and it troubled him that He might be real. At the same time he decided he was not prepared to give his entire life to God – that was, until he was involved in a serious car crash in 1983.

I met Ron Cantor for the first time in March 2011. We met in Tel Aviv and he shared his story and then the vision he has – the vision that drives him – which is potentially world-changing.

Ron takes up his story.

By 1983, aged seventeen, I was thinking a lot about God. In the autumn, when the time came for Yom Kippur, the holiest day of the Jewish year, when we try and obtain forgiveness for our sins, I decided to fast in the hope I would find God and the answers to some of my questions. Being brought up in a traditional Jewish family, I was used to going to the synagogue on Yom Kippur, but this was the first time I had fasted as well.

At the end of the twenty-four-hour fast I felt very hungry. I also felt spiritually empty and, what was most disappointing, I did not feel forgiven or any closer to God.

About a month later I was with another friend called Dean. He told me that he had been a believer in Jesus for a short time but, wanting to stay popular with his friends, he had given it all up. I was keen to know whether believing in Yeshua (Jesus) had made him happy and as we talked, he recognized that I was a Jewish guy searching for God and he felt it was his duty to help me! So he took me to see a movie about Yeshua which reduced both of us to tears. However, I knew the power of a well-written script and I was not going to start believing in Yeshua because a Hollywood producer made me cry.

But, as Dean was driving, I began to pray! This was the

first time in my life I had genuinely prayed. I told God that I now believed He was real and I wanted to know how to serve Him. "Show me what to do to serve you," I prayed. "Do I need to become an Orthodox Jew?" (At that time I had never heard of Messianic Judaism and did not know that there were Jews who believed in Yeshua.)

The next thing I remember, as we were driving round a bend in the road, Dean lost control of the car. I thought I was going to die. We swerved from side to side, spun out of control and landed upside down in a ditch. It was dark and there were no other cars on the road. We managed to climb out of the car. The car was wrecked but we were unhurt.

My mind was still on the prayer I had just prayed, telling God I believed He was real. How could He be real if we had just been involved in a car crash? I was about to find out.

We were surrounded by fields, in the middle of countryside, but there was one house nearby. We walked up the drive and knocked on the door, and a married couple opened the door and invited us in. Whilst the husband took Dean to use the telephone, the wife took me into the living room, where I immediately noticed a Bible and a magazine with an article about a man called Keith Green – a Jewish believer in Yeshua who had died a year earlier in a plane crash. Much to my surprise, this couple were believers in Yeshua!

Before I knew it, the wife was explaining to me the message of salvation – the gospel story. At first I didn't understand it. I said, "If Jesus was the Son of God, the Messiah, why didn't He get off the cross and prove it?" Again she tried to explain to me that He came to die for us, and she talked about blood and sacrifice and redemption, but it made no sense to me until the presence and power of God fell upon me at that moment. It was so strong, I have no human words to describe it, other than the word "electricity"; and even that falls short of explaining this "presence" I experienced at that moment, which I knew to be real. It was then I understood. I said, "I believe", and I left that house a new person. I had been born again. I knew my sins were forgiven.

For some time I wrestled with being Jewish and believing in Jesus. I didn't know if there were any other Jewish people in the world who believed in Jesus, and from what I had understood, to believe in Yeshua was to say, "I am no longer a Jew." I began to read the New Testament and was stunned to find that the writers were Jewish. Then one day I met a Jewish woman who was also a believer. "Yes, I used to be Jewish too," I told her. On hearing that, she put her finger in my face and said, "Don't you ever say that again! You will always be Jewish." And that was when I first understood there is no contradiction in being Jewish and believing in Jesus.

Whilst still living in America, Ron attended Christ for the Nations and Messiah Biblical Institute. He also met his wife, Elana, who is an Israeli. They worked in Florida during the time when a revival was happening in Pensacola. Ron describes that time.

Well, it was quite exciting. We visited the revival meetings several times. Since becoming a believer I had read a number of books telling the stories of the great revivals, and I longed to see something like this in our day. A good friend of mine, Dr Michael Brown (himself a key leader in the revival), called me after his first visit to Pensacola and I could hear in his voice that he was shaken. He said, "Ron, this is it. This is the real thing." So we did visit Pensacola at that time, and then several years later we were invited to join the staff, and we returned to teach in the Brownsville Revival School of Ministry. It was a real privilege not just to be in the midst of that revival but also to teach Jewish roots and Jewish history to the young people in my classes (which averaged 500 in each class). Those young people were hungry for God and hungry for revival but knew nothing about the Jewish roots of the gospel. One of those students was a man called Daniel Kolenda who has now become the President of CfaN (Christ for All Nations), the ministry that Reinhard Bonnke started. Little did I realize then that one of my students would be leading one of the largest evangelistic ministries in the world and that our paths would cross again in the future.

In 2003 Ron and Elana and their three children came to live in Israel. I asked Ron to explain his understanding of what God is doing in Israel today.

I would say He is opening the eyes of Israelis to recognize that Yeshua is the Messiah. He is fulfilling His word, which says the Jews will one day return to this land of Israel. But that is just the beginning of the story, because the vision described in Ezekiel 37 has two parts – the first part is about dry bones getting bodies, but they are still dead, and the second part is about those bodies coming to life. And today we are seeing Israelis returning to this land from all around the world. Many are being born again and the life of God is coming back into Jewish people living here.

But there is also a third phase. When Paul visited Pisidian

Antioch, he shared the gospel in the synagogue with the Jewish people living there. Some received his message whilst others did not. Paul's and Barnabas' response was: "We had to speak the word of God to you first. Since you reject it and do not consider yourselves worthy of eternal life, we now turn to the Gentiles. For this is what the Lord has commanded us: 'I have made you a light for the Gentiles, that you may bring salvation to the ends of the earth'" (Acts 13:46–47).

The Israeli body of believers has become dependent on people from other nations and having them pray for us and send us finances. But now, I believe, it is time for the body of believers in Israel to rise up and fulfil the calling that Paul quoted in Acts 13:47, when he referred to a verse in Isaiah 49:6 which says, "I have made you a light for the Gentiles, that you may bring salvation to the ends of the earth." So it is not enough that we only share the gospel with Israelis; we also have an anointing and a calling to go out from this nation to the nations of the world. Isaiah 2:3 says, "The law will go out from Zion, the word of the Lord from Jerusalem." So when we, a group of Israeli believers, get on an aeroplane at Ben Gurion airport and go to another nation in order to reach that nation with the gospel, we are fulfilling prophecy.

Through Daniel Kolenda, his former student who is now the leader of CfaN, Ron is now taking teams of young Israeli believers to Africa.

When I was in Africa the first time, I found it so amazing that when I came back I said, "God, I have to go back there. I love Israel but I can preach to more people in Africa in a weekend, than a year in Israel!" For many months I prayed and sought the Lord, and when I heard from a good friend of mine that this former student, Daniel Kolenda, had become the heir apparent of CfaN, I felt the Lord say, "There's your open door. Give him a call." So I did, and he invited me to come to one of their campaigns, really just to watch.

What I saw was phenomenal. The crowds! On our first night, the night before the campaign started, we were invited to a dinner in honour of Reinhard Bonnke, the founder of CfaN. As we drove up to the place where the meal was being held, I remember getting out of the car, and there were mobs of people there. These were not people who had been invited to this event – they had simply heard that Reinhard Bonnke was going to be there and they wanted to see him! It reminded me of what often happened to Jesus – when people heard He was in town they would mob Him. I thought I was going to get trampled. I was amazed at the eagerness of the people.

The next night, the first night of the campaign, over 300,000 people came to hear the gospel. The numbers increased over the five nights of the crusade, and by the end over 700,000 people were there. I saw blind eyes open and the lame walk; so many miracles!

On the first day in Africa I felt the Lord say to me that He was going to open up a door of opportunity. On the last day, on the way to the airport, I felt so happy because I had seen things I had previously only dreamt about seeing. However, no door had opened and I was an hour from the airport. So I said, "Lord, you said you were going to open up a door, and here I am, about to go home." All of a sudden, the man sitting next to me, a wonderful African pastor by the name of Mike Moses, turned to me and said, "Ron, I want you to come back to Africa and preach the gospel." So we began to make plans for a campaign in the future, and I thought how amazing it was that at the last minute, the Lord had opened up a door.

I left that place and flew to another city where I had to wait a whole day for my flight back to Israel. As I was waiting, I thought about this invitation and I had no peace of mind about it. I began to pray and asked God, "Why don't I have peace about this? You said you were going to open up a door and a door has opened, but I am uncomfortable." And He spoke to me. Now, I don't want you to get the wrong idea. I do not have an ongoing conversation with God – I wish I did – but there are moments and there are times when God speaks so clearly, and you just know in your heart that God has spoken to you.

He said, "Ron, if you come back to Nigeria and preach the gospel, that will be a great blessing for the people of Nigeria, but it will not touch Israel. But if you go back to Israel and put together a team of young Israeli believers and bring them with you as a delegation from Israel, not only will you be a blessing to Nigeria but you will bring blessing back to Israel."

As soon as I returned to Israel I shared this "vision" with some other Messianic Jewish leaders that I know and respect. Their spirits bore witness that this was right, and before we knew it, we had a team of eighteen young people ready to go to Africa. We went to Gombi in Nigeria, where for five nights we preached to literally tens of thousands of people. So many people gave their lives to the Lord! We saw blind eyes open and many other miracles. I was not the only person preaching; our whole team got involved.

We had a schoolteacher from Beit Shemesh who stood

up and preached her heart out! Afterwards she prayed for a blind woman, and the woman went home and suddenly realized that she could see! She came back the next night to testify to the young teacher who had prayed for her that once she was blind but now she could see!

And that was the goal – it wasn't about me and my ministry. Rather, it was about young Israelis coming and fulfilling their calling to be a light to the nations.

On our second trip we took a team to Hong in Nigeria. In five nights of campaign ministry, we received 67,000 decision cards – that is, people who decided they wanted to believe in Jesus! I don't know if there has ever been a larger evangelistic campaign going forth from Israel in history.

And what is the effect on their congregations in Israel when these young Israelis return and share these stories?

That's the double effect. It's not just that they go out to Africa and are a blessing there. When they come back here they are bolder – their faith has risen. I remember, when we got back, one young fellow had a friend whose fiancée (an unbeliever) had been diagnosed with cancer. Immediately he said, "I have to go and pray for her." Living in Israel as a believer can be intimidating. But those returning from Nigeria had more boldness, more willingness to step out in faith, and they didn't care as much about what people thought about them. We are taking another team soon and we expect the same thing – that they will come back changed, and that they will never forget what happens to them in Africa, and that they will impart these things into the congregations in Israel.

As you look ahead to the next few years, what are you anticipating?

We believe that as we fulfil the calling of God to be a light to the nations, grace is released on Israel and more Israelis come to faith. We are not the only ones doing this – there are other leaders in Israel who have embraced this vision. They are going to other nations of the world, including India. Together we are the restored remnant of Israel – we have to be a light to the nations. We will not rest until we see what is written in the book of Acts happening in Israel.

Chapter 5
Maron and Angelika Raheb

Maron Raheb was born and brought up in the Old City of Jerusalem where violence, crime, drug taking and drug dealing were commonplace. Today he is married to Angelika (who is German), and together they are encouraging new believers in both Jerusalem and the West Bank and starting new churches. They are pioneers.

A few years ago, when I first met Maron, he had just recovered from being a drug addict. In fact, his life had changed out of all recognition. This came about through a chance meeting with a man he had previously sold drugs to. But when Maron met him on this occasion, he was no longer interested in taking drugs – in fact, he was no longer a drug addict. Maron was staggered at the change in his appearance and even more staggered when he heard that "the Lord" had set him free from drugs. And so it was that Maron took advice from his friend and went to The House of Victory drug and alcohol rehabilitation centre in Haifa, founded by David and Karen Davis. Whilst he was there, not only was the power of addiction broken in his life, but he became a Christian too. The House of Victory helps both Jews and Arabs together, so, as this story reveals, Maron's hatred and bitterness towards Jewish people were challenged to the core.

This is the story of two people from very different backgrounds who found each other in the Old City of Jerusalem, almost by chance. It is a story of divine appointments, faith and courage. It is a story of an emerging generation of young believers living in Israel today who are working to realize biblical prophecy.

Recently Maron and Angelika invited me to visit them in their apartment, which is situated on the outskirts of Jerusalem. I was there to hear about all the developments in their work. But Maron started by sharing just how grateful he is to God for saving him from his old way of life and certain death.

That my life has changed is all because of the grace and love of the Lord. He has opened many doors of opportunity for me. We are just tools in His hand and He wants to use us to win more souls for His Kingdom and to bring more glory to His name. We are disciples of the Lord Jesus; we are His ambassadors representing the Kingdom of God here in this world. We have a big responsibility as believers to go from place to place to serve Him and even to start churches. I believe this is our responsibility, and God is calling us to work more and more to bring more people into His Kingdom.

Maron and Angelika have three young children. They have chosen to live in a Jewish neighbourhood in a suburb of Jerusalem. I asked him why.

The Lord has healed my heart of bitterness and hatred towards the Jewish people. Before I gave my life to Jesus Christ, I was full of hatred. I grew up in the Old City, and when I was a child my parents and the people around me told me that the Jews were our enemies and we needed to get revenge, because they took our land by force, and so we must retake the land by force and fight against them. In addition to this, I once had a bad experience when several Israeli soldiers beat me up very severely and I was left badly injured. As a result, hatred and bitterness filled my heart and I could not forget what had happened.

When I gave my life to Jesus Christ I was a recovering drug addict. I was receiving treatment at The House of Victory in Haifa, and when I first went there I saw something that shocked me – Jews and Arabs together in the same building, living together, speaking together, praying together. This shocked me so much, I felt I could not stay there and decided to leave the following day. But that night, they were meeting to pray together and one of the men came over to pray for me. When I discovered that he was Jewish, my heart melted and I asked the Lord to heal me of all the bitterness and hatred in my life and to give me His love for the Jews. Immediately the Lord performed a miracle in my life, and He filled me with love, and I started to hug everybody! I was able to hug the Jewish guy who had prayed for me and I felt such joy. So from that time I decided to be a man of reconciliation and to build relationships with Jewish people. When I returned to Jerusalem after being in Haifa, I met some Messianic Jewish pastors and we started to meet to talk and pray together. And here we are today, living in a Jewish neighbourhood where all my neighbours are Jewish, and they are all wonderful people!

I believe it is important that I can show love to everybody, regardless of whether they are Jewish or Palestinian. It makes me really happy to know that our Jewish neighbours accept us here. It is wonderful. We always greet each other. Angelika and I try to be the aroma of Christ in our neighbourhood. We know we are God's ambassadors here and we long to share the gospel with those we live amongst.

We were sat drinking tea and enjoying a delicious apple flan that Angelika had made. Maron talked about his passion to share the gospel with as many people as possible, because he believes the time is short. Today he and Angelika are active evangelists working with whoever comes across their path, particularly in the West Bank amongst the Palestinian people.

At the beginning of 2011, I felt the Lord was telling me that I was to share the message of salvation with everybody I met, because He was coming back very soon. As I look at what is going on around us, with the economic situation, the unrest in the Arab nations and the challenges that Israel is facing, I realize these are signs that Jesus' return will happen soon. I believe He is encouraging us to work harder to make the Kingdom of God known to as many people as possible in order to win more souls for Him. I remember the words of Jesus to His disciples before He ascended into heaven: "you will receive power when the Holy Spirit comes on you; and you will be my witnesses in Jerusalem, and in all Judea and Samaria, and to the ends of the earth" (Acts 1:8). Jesus has given us the power to do this work through the Holy Spirit; we are equipped, so we must preach the gospel!

So yes, I am working as an evangelist. I believe it is very important that we must be willing to speak to everyone, whether they are Jews or Muslims or Christians. If we are servants of the Lord, we must be willing to speak to anybody without prejudice.

And so Maron spends his days travelling from place to place. One day finds him in Jerusalem; the next day he could be somewhere in the West Bank.

I can only speak for myself, but I don't like being a fish in a small pool! I prefer being like a butterfly, flying from place to place. I believe it is my calling to reach people everywhere, not just in Jerusalem but also in the West Bank – and, praise God, He is doing mighty things among the people there. There is a lot of interest in Jesus and who He really is. People are coming to our meetings and they have many questions, and there is a real hunger for spiritual truth. However, it is slow work and it takes time before we see results, but I am so happy to be doing this work. Despite the difficulties we face, I have peace and joy in my heart and a great sense of freedom.

Maron has described how the people are hungry to hear the truth about God, so does he believe the unrest amongst many Arab nations of the world is creating a window of opportunity for the gospel to be preached in these countries?

There is no simple answer to that question; I can answer "yes" and "no". Here in Israel, despite showing some initial interest in spiritual matters, many people shrug their shoulders and tell me they just want to get on with their work and live their own lives. Here there are many spiritual forces controlling the people – for example, the spirits of religion and Islam. These spiritual forces are trying to hinder the work of God in this land. But, on the other hand, I also see many people who are really hungry and they want to know more about God.

Muslims read about Jesus in the Koran, where it describes the miracles that He performed. They are interested to know more about Jesus, and many Muslims are accepting the whole truth about Him, that He is the Son of God, and they are believing in Him as their Saviour. I know that this is happening not just here in Israel and the West Bank, but also in Egypt and Lebanon and other Arab countries. I am hearing reports of many Muslims receiving Jesus into their lives.

We need Christians in the rest of the world to pray that the Lord would bring more workers into this country, because as Jesus Himself said, "The harvest is plentiful, but the workers are few. Ask the Lord of the harvest, therefore, to send out workers into his harvest field" (Luke 10:2). So we need people who have a calling from God to come and work with us here in the Middle East, especially in Israel. We are also praying that more local people will start to serve Him in this way, because the Arabs need Arabs and the Jews need Jews to speak to each other effectively. We need a revival amongst the servants who are already here, so that we can start to work even harder to win more souls for the Kingdom of God.

Angelika, as a single young woman, chose to leave the comfort of living in Germany to work in Israel. Her story is very interesting, not least because of the unhappy history between Germany and Israel as a result of the Holocaust. She explained how she ended up in Israel.

Well, I think it started on the day I gave my life to the Lord. I said to Him, "You can do with my life what you want to do." I had always had connections with Israel through an aunt who moved here many years ago to start a new life. I remember coming here, when I was young, for a holiday. So I grew up familiar with the Jewish people; but I knew nothing about the story of the Arabs. So when I gave my life to the Lord I said to Him, "What is the plan that you have for me?" In order to learn more about the Lord, I went to Bible School and then went on a mission trip, on a boat, around Greece. For one year we were sailing on that boat, from island to island, until we reached Turkey. And it was in Turkey that, for the first time, I got to know Muslim people, and I realized their need of knowing a Saviour. And that was when the Lord started to stir my heart about Muslim people, the Middle East and focusing on a completely different people group.

I asked Angelika how she met Maron.

That was much later. By then I had moved to Israel and I was living in the Old City, where I was working with women in need. I had been here for three years and really felt that this was the place where God wanted me to be. But the apartment where I lived was terrible. It was all I could afford with the money I had, but because it was in such a bad condition, I knew it would only last over the summer. The windows did not close. It had no bathroom, no stove and no refrigerator. As winter approached I realized I needed to move.

So I asked the Lord for two things – a different apartment and a husband! I wanted a husband with whom I could work in the Middle East. I fasted for one week and at the end of the fast I felt the Lord say to me, "Today is the day you will move. Today is the day I will open the door."

As usual, I went out to visit the ladies in the Old City and one of them said to me, "My neighbour has just finished renovating an apartment on the top of the roof. Why don't you go and see it?" So I went up there and, compared to my little room, it was a dream. I asked the lady how much the rent was and she told me 500 dollars – that was double the amount I was currently paying. So I told her I couldn't afford it and left.

When I got back to my apartment, as soon as I opened the door, my pastor from Germany called me. He said, "Angelika, we have just had a committee meeting and we have decided to raise your support by 250 dollars." That was exactly the answer I needed, so I rushed back to the lady and said, "I will take that apartment!"

It was on the way back that I saw Maron. At that time I didn't know him well – I just knew that he loved the Lord and was studying at a Bible college. He said to me, "Is there anything I can help you with?" At first I thought, "No, I don't need any help." But then I realized that I had to move! So I said to him that if he could organize for some guys from the church to help me move, that would be great.

Three days later he came with some men from the church and they helped me to move all my belongings. It was after this that he invited me to go with him to Ramlah to preach at a meeting for ladies in three weeks' time. I agreed, and after the service we were sitting together in his relatives' house, and he said to me, "I really wonder why you are not married." He started to share his testimony and his vision and his heart. And he said, "In the last three weeks God has been speaking to me about you being my future wife."

I was completely shocked! I wasn't shocked in a negative way – it was just that things were happening rather fast. But because I had asked the Lord for those two things, a new flat and a husband, I felt the Holy Spirit speaking into my heart, "This is my answer."

So I said to Maron, "Give me three days to pray about this." I felt so much the peace of the Lord about this, and three months later we were engaged, and three months after that we were married. And then together, we started our ministry.

What may seem surprising is that Maron, an Arab, and Angelika, a German, have chosen to live in a Jewish suburb of Jerusalem. Angelika continued:

For fifteen years, I had lived on the Arab side of Jerusalem because my original calling had been to the Arab people. So when we moved to the Jewish side, to begin with I felt as though I had walked away from my calling. But I have come to realize that the heart of the Jewish people is very open; it is not as hard as I thought it would be. We have always had good relationships with Jewish people – not just Messianic Jews but ordinary Jewish people.

Before I came into the country the Lord gave me a picture – I have just remembered it. It was a picture of myself sitting on top of the Western Wall with one leg on the Arab side and the other leg on the Jewish side. And that picture perfectly describes our life and situation here: we are standing with one foot in the Arab side and the other foot in the Jewish side, and we are trying to show Jesus to them both.

As well as working alongside Maron as an evangelist, Angelika is mother to their three young children. So how does she manage to divide her time between being a wife, a mother and a "pioneer" alongside her husband?

Yes, our main calling is to pioneer new ministry in this land. There are not many people who are doing that. Whilst it is a risky and adventurous calling, it is our heartfelt desire to reach out to the unreached. And yes, we have three young children and I spend much of my time teaching them – in fact, my main priority right now is my kids, because I feel they need me as a mother. We do not want them to grow up and say, "Our parents were too busy on the mission field to have any time for us." However, I try to combine both family and ministry. I give as much time as I can to working alongside Maron and I go with him on outreaches. We share everything together.

Everything we do starts in a very small way, which at first can be very frustrating. But when we see more people coming along, then we get more excited about the project. At the same time, I am very encouraged about some of the work we have been doing for a long time – for example, the Bethlehem ministry. These are people we have known for many years and we can see how much they have grown and developed. But we also see their needs.

We are now also reaching out to different people groups and people of different backgrounds; we need a lot of wisdom for that. But when you see the sparkle in the eye of a person when he is introduced to Jesus, when he gets excited about the good news – this is what excites us most.

It sometimes feels lonely, because not everybody has the heart of a pioneer. In fact, not many people like to pioneer. Most people like to stay in a situation in which they feel comfortable and don't want to move away from that position. Pioneering means you have to jump into a new situation with new people in a new environment with challenges, and maybe with people not liking you, or people putting obstacles in front of your feet. But eventually, pioneering something new means fruit, and this is what we all like to see.

I hope and pray that those people who give their life to the Lord become strong. I don't mean just being believers. I mean people who know they have a destiny from the Lord and who learn to hear the voice of the Lord. I believe it is vitally important that we learn to hear His voice. And I wish this for the Arab people – that they start to hear His voice, and move and push through all the obstacles that often cross their paths, because ministering here is a battle. This is not a place for weak people; rather, it is for people who are ready to stand up, people who are born to be heroes.

We want to get out and find the hero in the Arab – that person who has grown up in a very neglected setting, maybe with parents who did not love him – who is suddenly finding and embracing the love of Jesus. We want to help him persevere and leave the past behind, so that he is no longer living with a poverty mentality, but rather saying, "I am a child of God and I inherit all the riches He has for me." We want to help that person run the race and reach the finishing line.

Chapter 6
Peter and Yarden Nasser

Some marriages are so unusual – unlikely, even – that they can only be described as "made in heaven". Whilst the number of mixed-race marriages is increasing in the UK and the US, it is still unusual for an Arab to marry a Jew, especially in Israel.

Peter and Yarden Nasser are even more unusual. Not only is theirs a mixed-race marriage – Peter is an Arab and Yarden is Jewish – but they are both working for the missionary organization *Jews for Jesus* in Israel. I met them at the *Jews for Jesus* headquarters in Tel Aviv.

Peter was born in an Arab village called Kfar Samea in northern Israel, a three-hour drive from Tel Aviv. The village is home to a mixed population of Druze people and nominal Christians. Peter described what it was like for him growing up in this environment.

My parents came to faith before I was born and we went, as a family, to an evangelical church. Since it was an entirely Arab village, I grew up only knowing the Arab culture, which meant I didn't meet many Jewish people. I went to an Arab school, we shopped in Arab markets, and all my friends were Arabs.

As I was growing up, my ambition was to travel the world. The Arab culture is a very closed community and it's very hard to leave. So my dream was to learn more, to be free from this community and to be somebody important!

When I was young my attitude towards Jewish people was non-existent because I was so isolated from them and their culture. But when I was eighteen I left home and moved to Tel Aviv to study, and it was there I started to interact with Jewish people. That was when I realized there was a problem between Jews and Arabs. Until then I had heard occasional news reports about disturbances and heard some stories about violence and conflict, but because I had not had any personal involvement, I hadn't reacted in any way. But aged eighteen, in Tel Aviv, I started to feel the hatred from Jewish people towards me personally, and so my response was to hate them back. As time went on I grew to hate all that Israel represented and decided that I would like to leave the country and see the world.

So I started to travel. I went to Switzerland, because I had some friends there, and stayed for a year. It was there I almost got married, but the relationship didn't last and after a year we broke up. I was really upset and angry with God for allowing this to happen. I knew it was time to leave Switzerland but I didn't want to go back to Israel. I wanted to find somewhere where I could live my life in a quiet, simple and peaceful way, so I moved to Australia. I had been promised a job there by a man I thought I could trust. But he stole my money and possessions, and I found myself in Sydney, alone with nothing.

It was there I met a missionary called Jonathan who was from England. I was feeling extremely lonely, my thoughts were in turmoil and I was smoking heavily. When I met Jonathan I noticed something different about him. Although people didn't particularly like what he was doing in Australia, he still had a love for them. And there was something else I noticed – he was a man at peace with himself. So I started talking to him and asked him about his life, and how it was that he was so happy and content. His answer was so simple – "Jesus."

"I know about Jesus," I replied. "I've been to church, but I have never experienced the peace you have found."

He replied, "Well, you have to know Jesus personally; it's not enough to know *about* Jesus."

At first I didn't understand what he meant. But over the next six months we became good friends, and as we travelled around Australia together he taught me from the Bible.

I would talk to him about the problems I experienced in life. He would listen and try to encourage me to become a Christian, but I couldn't believe everything he told me about Jesus – something always held me back. I suppose I was trying to sort out my own life in my own way. So in an effort to find what or who I was looking for, I left Australia and moved to New Zealand.

I had a brother who lived there and so I stayed with him. At first life was good and I thought I had found what I was looking for. But as days turned into weeks, I could not find a job and became discouraged, until eventually I passed the time by spending hours every day on the internet. My brother suggested that instead of wasting my time on the computer, I should start reading. He gave me a pile of books and one of them was a Bible. For the first time in my life I sat down and started to read it. It wasn't long before I realized how far away I was from being able to call myself a Christian.

So I prayed and confessed my sins, and my life changed instantly. I had just read the words of Jesus, "Come to me, all you who are weary and burdened, and I will give you rest. Take my yoke upon you and learn from me, for I am gentle and humble in heart, and you will find rest for your souls. For my yoke is easy and my burden is light" (Matthew 11:28–30). And that is what happened – all my hatred towards Israel and the Jewish people and all the memories of my suffering disappeared, and God replaced those things with His joy and His peace.

I told my brother, "Do you know, I really have love for the Jewish people." It felt strange at first, because I really had hated and despised these people before, and certainly did not want anything to do with them.

It was soon after this experience that I returned to Israel. I didn't really know what I was going to do or, indeed, what I wanted to do. I started going to a church and joined a team that went out evangelizing on the streets, and that was where I met Yarden, who is now my wife – my Jewish wife! She was evangelizing and I was evangelizing, and we started to evangelize together, and three years later we were married. During those three years we met with the leaders of *Jews for Jesus* and started to work with them, and now we are both on their staff!

When I told my parents I was going to marry a Jewish girl, my father was concerned because he had seen how much I had hated living in Israel and hated being amongst Jewish people. He reminded me that if I married a Jewish girl and lived in Israel, our children would be Israeli and they would be expected to serve in the army. He tried to make me realize that Yarden was not "one of our own" and that I would have to give up my Arab culture and adopt the Jewish way of life, with all their traditions. It took over a year before my father was persuaded that actually Yarden was a believer, just like "us". It is still unusual for an Arab to marry a Jew; Arabs generally do not like the idea of being involved with Jewish people at such close proximity. But now everything is good between us and my father has accepted Yarden.

As for how Yarden's parents reacted to us wanting to get married – her father is a secular Jew, and he wasn't that concerned about it. At first I had problems with her mum! But now everything is good.

When we go out onto the streets wearing our *Jews for Jesus* T-shirts, Jewish people find it odd when they meet me. They recognize that I am an Arab and they often respond by saying to me, "You are an Arab, but why would you want to come to us and talk about Jesus?"

Other Jewish people tell me to leave them alone and go instead and talk to the Palestinians about Jesus. I usually reply by saying to them, "Don't worry, there are people talking to the Palestinians about Jesus, but I am here to tell you."

"Why would you do such a thing?" they ask me. "Why do you care about us?"

So I tell them my story and about the love God has put in my heart for them. That makes them curious and then they want to know more about Jesus and salvation. It is really a blessing for me, an Arab, to share Jesus with Jewish people. At a time when the conflict between Arabs and Jews is so deep, the Jewish people I meet are usually extremely interested to talk about why I, an Arab, want to talk to them about their Jewish Messiah.

It was time to talk to Yarden. Born in the Ukraine into a secular Jewish family, she came to Israel when she was fifteen years old – alone. Yarden's story is the portrait of an independent young woman determined to find her true identity and discover her destiny.

I came to Israel on a programme called *Na'alay*, which brings Jewish youth to Israel from around the world. I decided I wanted to emigrate to Israel, so I came when I was fifteen years old and was accepted by an Orthodox Jewish high school in Tel Aviv for the final three years of my education.

Three years later my family came to Israel. But they didn't settle and decided to go back to the Ukraine, leaving me here on my own.

When I first arrived, I was very excited. I was independent and was where I wanted to be, doing what I wanted to do! Whilst I was in the country of my people, Israel, the culture was different to what I had been used to, and gradually, without the emotional support of my family around me and without people who could help me to solve the problems I began to face, life became hard.

Although my parents were secular Jews, when I was seven years old my paternal grandmother started to take me to a Jewish community centre to learn about the Jewish holidays (Hannukah, Passover, etc.) and what they mean. At that time I also started to learn Hebrew. So before I came to Israel I could speak and read Hebrew.

When I came to Israel, I lived with an Orthodox family

and had to join in with the requirements of leading a religious Jewish life. Despite coming from a secular family, I had read a lot of books about Judaism whilst I was still living in the Ukraine, so I was well prepared. However, when I started attending the Orthodox school, I found it much stricter than I had imagined. What I found hard to understand was that people blindly followed traditions without question; they did not appear to have a conviction stemming from a deep relationship with God. It appeared to me that they really didn't understand the deeper meaning about why they followed so many rules to the letter of the law. And it was this aspect that shocked me.

I found myself asking them, "How can you do these things if you don't understand why you do them?"

"We are following tradition," they would reply.

However, it was during those three years at an Orthodox school that I came to know Jesus as my personal Saviour and Lord. During my first two summer holidays I went home to visit my parents in the Ukraine. By the time I came back to start my third and final year at school, I had started to question a lot of things.

When I was seven, at the same time as my grandmother had started taking me to the Jewish community centre to learn more about Judaism, my mother had come to faith in Jesus. She too started to teach me – about Jesus. But at that time I didn't understand about Him being a Saviour – I just thought He was a good person and a friend of children! I couldn't understand then the concept that He came to die for my personal sins.

Now, aged seventeen and at a religious school in Israel, I studied about the Messiah from a Jewish perspective.

Consequently, I found myself asking a lot of questions. Why was it that my mum believed Jesus was the Messiah, but here in Israel they believed something different about Him? I started to wonder whether there was any connection between Judaism and Christianity. I had heard that Jesus was also called "Christ", which means "Messiah". But was this just His family name?

We also had classes comparing the three major religions of the world – Judaism, Islam and Christianity. During these lessons I could see that the things they were saying about Jesus were wrong and were purely based on prejudice rather than the facts. As I questioned the rabbis who taught us, they could not answer my questions. So, in desperation, when nobody was watching, I would use the internet to find out as much as I could about the Messiah. I researched what both the Old Testament and the New Testament had to say about Him.

On *Shabbat* (the Sabbath) in Orthodox families and schools, many things are forbidden. For example, you are not allowed to switch on the lights. You are not allowed to draw or write or do homework. You can only eat, pray and sleep! I often felt stressed about this; I hated not being able to do anything.

One *Shabbat*, I was feeling bored, I didn't know what to do and I had so many questions, so I opened the Bible (I had only the Old Testament) and read Isaiah chapter 53. Suddenly, here I was, reading the prophecy about the suffering servant, and I realized it was describing Jesus. I took the chapter to show my room-mates and asked them what they thought about it. One of the other girls agreed with me that it seemed to be describing Jesus. But she threw the Bible on the bed and accused me of reading the New Testament. "No," I replied, "this is an Old Testament from the synagogue." Even she could see it was a prophecy about Jesus.

This experience challenged me to dig even deeper and I looked for more prophecies about the Messiah. Little by little, I realized that Jesus was the only one who could fulfil all those prophecies. Later I started reading other books and came to understand that Jesus died to save us from our personal sins and that I needed Jesus in my life.

One day, I was praying and feeling very lonely, because I felt as though I was the only Jewish person who believed in Jesus in Israel. When I had finished praying I went out for a walk and passed by somebody who was giving out invitations to a concert at a local Messianic congregation in Kfar Saba, just a short drive out of Tel Aviv. I found my way to that concert and there I met a lot of Jewish believers in Jesus who shared their testimonies with me and encouraged me. I started going to that congregation regularly, even though I was still attending an Orthodox Jewish school, and it was there that I started growing in my faith.

At the end of my third and final year at school I had to take an oral examination and answer questions about Judaism in front of a rabbi. He asked me a lot of questions about my Jewish background, Jewish practices and Jewish holidays. After I had answered all his questions he started to ask me about Jesus and what I thought about Him – was He the truth or a lie? I was surprised that he started asking me these things, but I told him that I believed Jesus was true. He was shocked at my answer and wanted to know how I had reached this conclusion. I explained to him and showed him the prophecies in the Old Testament that had persuaded me that Jesus is the promised Messiah of Israel.

After that I had several further meetings with him to discuss these things, and in the end he told me he was sorry, but he could not allow me to pass the test in Judaism, and that it would be hard for me to stay in Israel if I chose to believe in Jesus. He added that I therefore had to decide between Judaism or Christianity. I replied that I could see that Judaism is based on biblical principles found in the Old Testament, but also there are prophecies and promises of God to His nation which have been fulfilled by Jesus. I explained that I could see no contradiction between Judaism and Christianity – rather, one is a continuation of the other.

I could see it was hard for this rabbi to understand my thinking and beliefs. Anticipating this, I had earlier prepared for him a list of biblical prophecies to do with Jesus, drawn from both the Old and the New Testaments. As I gave the list to him, he took the piece of paper from my hand and hid it in his pocket.

And so I graduated from school and began my national service working in a health clinic for a year. During this time I moved to Hadera and started going to a local church where I volunteered to help in my spare time. It was there that I began to get involved with other believers in evangelism. One day the pastor of the church invited me to help at a New Age festival in Acco. We were giving out books and sharing with the people about Jesus.

And it was through helping at these annual festivals in Acco that I met my husband Peter. We found ourselves evangelizing together; he was witnessing to Jews and I was witnessing to Arabs! I needed some help with translation into Arabic, so I went to Peter and asked him some questions. I saw him witnessing to a group of Jewish people and found it interesting that he was witnessing to them about his personal relationship with their God and Messiah. That excited me. He helped me with the translation into Arabic, and later we talked and shared our testimonies and started getting to know each other.

I loved going out and talking to people, giving them literature and sharing my faith. I spent most of my free time going to the New Age festivals, which attracted large numbers of Jewish people with spiritual hunger. This was how I first met a *Jews for Jesus* group. They were at one of the New Age festivals, where they had a booth. They were giving away books for free and were wearing *Jews for Jesus* T-shirts!

Regarding Peter, I was brought up not to distinguish between Gentiles and Jews. In my family there were people who had married non-Jews, so this was not a problem for me. My family has always been very open-minded. In fact, when I was young, my father brought me to Israel for the first time, and he joked then that one day I might marry an Arab! But I never imagined myself marrying an Arab. Rather, I expected to marry somebody Jewish – most likely from a Russian background similar to mine.

When I was studying in the Orthodox school, the culture there was very anti-Arab. We were surrounded by Arab villages and sometimes we were threatened by people from the neighbourhood. The director of our school used to say that if he saw a girl going out with or even talking to an Arab boy, she would be expelled from the school. So I was very afraid to talk to Arab boys. As a new immigrant, I couldn't distinguish between Jews and Israeli Arabs, because they all looked the same to me! So I was very careful not to have any contact with Arabs. However, when I came to faith everything changed, because I was meeting believers from all sorts of different backgrounds – even Arabs!

I became very interested in Christian Arabs because, despite the suicide bombings and acts of terrorism that were happening frequently at that time, I was hearing stories of Muslims who were coming to faith and being born again. I found this very exciting. I knew that if a Jewish person came to faith, they would be cut off from their community and their relatives would be upset; but even so, nobody would kill them. But I knew that if a Muslim came to faith in Jesus, they could be killed. I was so interested in this that I started going to an Arabic church in Shefar'am in order to get to know some Christian people from an Arabic background. Later, as we got to know each other, we evangelized together. So when I met Peter, I was used to being with Arabs. But when he asked me to marry him, I knew that Arab people, even Christians, have their own traditions and that we could experience problems.

Now I am very excited that my Arab husband is working for *Jews for Jesus* amongst Jewish people. He shares his story with so many Jewish people and he tells them he is married to a Jew. Likewise, when I share my story I tell people how Jesus broke down the wall of hostility between Jews and Gentiles, or Jews and Arabs, on the cross to make peace, and that we can be reconciled. This is the answer to all the trouble – if you have Jesus in your heart, you can have peace with people and peace with God.

When I visit Peter's family in their village in Galilee, I witness to the Arabs who live there. I feel this is the calling for the rest of my life.

Chapter 7
Joshua Pex

Joshua Pex is a lawyer in Jerusalem. He specializes in issues to do with social justice, human rights and religious freedom in Israel. This story reveals how his awareness of these challenging aspects of life started and how he and his wife Sarah, a social worker, have found a way of helping women involved in modern-day slavery.

I met Joshua at his law firm and he started by telling me a little about his background and upbringing.

I was born in the south of Israel in Eilat. Both of my parents immigrated to Israel as young adults. My mother is American – she came in the early 1970s – and my father is Dutch. Only my mother is Jewish. Both of them were travelling independently around the world and happened to be in the Sinai Desert at the same time. In those days the Sinai was part of Israel and many people who were looking for the meaning of life and God found themselves in the Sinai. My parents were among them and in a miraculous way, although they were both very far from God, they were seeking meaning to life and seeking God. They were looking in many different places but when they received Bibles and started to read them, they received Jesus into their hearts in a very simple way.

My mother describes how she was reading the New Testament and fell in love with Jesus, and she was certain she was the first Jewish person to believe in Jesus since the days of the Apostles. But slowly she discovered there were other believers, and together they formed a community in Eilat, where my parents remain until today. They have a youth hostel, which is where I grew up together with my three siblings, situated on the beach in Eilat in a very international community. There were always many guests from all over the world.

When I was eighteen I joined the army. Like almost all young Israelis, I was drafted for three years. After that time I travelled for a while before starting at Law School, which was not what I was expecting! Even my father said, "Why are you going to study law?" It didn't seem to fit with my personality. But I had always been interested in justice and social change, and I really went to study law with the idea that law can be a very powerful tool to bring change to society.

I grew up in an environment that was very supportive of the faith. Our parents used to read the Bible to my siblings and I. We would pray together and worship. However, I have to say that it was only when I was older that I rededicated my life to the faith, because when you are a child you go along with what your parents teach you, but when you grow up you go through difficult challenges. Perhaps it was the years I served in the military that caused me to feel very insecure about many things in life. You have to question whether what you hear from your parents is true – especially in Israel, where a Jewish person having faith in Jesus is such an offence – an unacceptable thing that upsets many people, because it seems like a betrayal of your people and Judaism.

Many Jewish people do not believe that you can be Jewish and believe in Jesus at the same time. "That is for Christians, not for Jews," they say.

But as I grew older, particularly in the years after the military, I rededicated myself to the faith.

I met my wife, Sarah, when I was a student at Law School. Even in the early days when we were just dating, I would hear her talking about her work with street people, especially women in prostitution, most of them addicted to drugs. I had always been interested in issues of human rights and law, but this particular issue was something that I had little experience of and, like many other people in Israel, I had heard very little about this phenomenon. If you are not in the right places, this whole issue is suppressed.

I was impressed by what Sarah was doing and the calling she had and the heart she had for these women. When she took me on a tour of the red light areas in the heart of Tel Aviv (there is a particular neighbourhood which is like a slum, close to an affluent area where there are skyscrapers), I was shocked to see these people on the streets. There was a tangible atmosphere of violence and fear. I saw drug addicts walking around like zombies and men walking around, openly looking for prostitutes, some of whom looked like walking skeletons – their bodies wasted away by sickness, drugs, violence and malnutrition. I asked myself how could it be that these things were going on in Israel. These sights sank into my heart and I felt a certain burden to do something, but didn't know what.

After I graduated and we got married, I became a lawyer, and at the back of my mind there was always the feeling that something needed to be done to help these women. But I was a lawyer and not a social worker. By this time we were also aware that sex trafficking was a major issue in Tel Aviv and gradually, through Sarah's work, we realized there was a need for legal assistance for some of these women.

A typical story involved a woman from the former Soviet Union who had grown up in difficult circumstances – let's call her Yelena. As a child Yelena had been abused, and as she grew up she become involved in bad relationships. Through one of her boyfriends she heard it would be possible to go to a Western country, where she could work taking care of old people and make a living so that she could support some of her family.

I found out that many similar women who came to Israel in the late 1990s were lured into this trap. They were brought to Egypt and then smuggled into Israel, through the desert, across the border illegally. On the way they would be beaten and raped so that by the time they arrived in Tel Aviv they would be exhausted. In Tel Aviv they would be sold like merchandise to their pimps and enslaved into prostitution.

Yelena was locked in an apartment and forced into sex with up to twelve men each day. The pimp told her she would be paid sometime in the future, but for now she had to pay her debt to him for buying her. She was alone, without papers, an illegal immigrant, defenceless and frightened. After a while, one of her clients decided that he liked her and would like to buy her from the pimp. Thinking life couldn't get any worse, she agreed and was bought for a few thousand dollars. But the man who bought her was very abusive and her situation became even worse. She became pregnant by this man and gave birth to a baby boy who is now five years old.

After a while, the relationship with this man ended

when he was arrested on criminal charges. Yelena decided to return to a life of prostitution – it was the only way she knew of making enough money to care for herself and her son. I have observed other, similar stories where sometimes these women adopt the stigma that society labels them with.

And that's when Sarah met Yelena a few years ago in one of the brothels. At first she wasn't interested in talking and told Sarah that she was there of her own free will, doing what she wanted to do and earning enough money to take care of her son. But as Sarah met her on a more regular basis, Yelena opened up to her and told her about her childhood and then how she had come to Israel, as a victim of human trafficking, although she didn't use those terms.

Over a period of two to three years Sarah persuaded her to leave prostitution and found a shelter for her, and that's where she is today. She has a job as a cleaner in a community centre. It's hard work, and she is only earning the minimum wage, but she is content. She takes her son to school every day and she is in a totally different place in life. To talk to her today, you find you are talking to an assertive person who knows who she is. The only problem is that she has no status in Israel, although her son is obviously an Israeli. The other problem is, she contracted Hepatitis C, so she is sick with a disease that could be very dangerous for her health and she needs to continue receiving the right treatment – something that would not happen if she went back to Moldova.

So we are hoping to gain legal status for her in Israel. It won't be easy but we do have experience in this field of immigration. Just one month ago the Israeli committee for humanitarian issues granted her temporary residence, which gives her governmental medical care and social security.

Yelena is in the process of moving out of the shelter. Her life has changed and now she is at a new start. It won't be easy for her being on her own, but she has taken responsibility for her life and wants to get on with a normal lifestyle outside the shelter.

Although the rate of trafficking has now slowed down, due to government legislation, there are many women in this position in Israel. The State of Israel has made good progress in eradicating this illegal practice of trafficking women from outside Israel into the country. But on the other hand, there is still a lot of "internal trafficking" – women who are Israelis but who are being trafficked and pimped within the country. We have to understand that slavery is a lucrative business; human traffickers do not care where the women come from as long as they are in control and have possession. It is more difficult for the police to enforce the law in the area of internal trafficking because the issue of slavery and control is more difficult to prove.

Sarah and I have started a charity called NOA (Not Objects Anymore). When we started the project, Sarah and I had a dream that we would find a way of providing legal assistance to these women. We were praying about it and without asking, we received a generous donation which enabled us to get started. Although I work as a lawyer in a commercial law firm in Israel and most of my work has to do with civil legal issues, the work with NOA currently takes up about 20 per cent of my time. As time goes on, our hope is that I will be able to spend more of my time devoted to helping these women, because that is where my heart is.

One of our aims is to try to change the overall picture by introducing changes in our legislation. We say sometimes, it's important to fight the mosquitoes, but it's more effective to drain the swamps. So we are working currently in three areas. The first is the ongoing legal representation of individuals who are referred to us by different organizations. Secondly, we have an emergency fund for these women who need small sums, which to them are very big sums, to pay certain bills. And thirdly, along with other similar-minded organizations, such as the Jerusalem Freedom Foundation, we are lobbying the Knesset, the Israeli parliament, concerning human trafficking, to try to pass a law that will criminalize the clients.

In Israel, as in many other countries, prostitution is not illegal. We hope that by making it illegal we will reduce the demand and also send out a message that it is morally wrong. Studies show that countries that have gone in this direction, like Sweden, have seen a big change in this area.

We also realize that it is not enough to pass a law; you also need to change the awareness of people through education, especially the awareness of men as to what this does to women. This is our dream at the moment.

Further information about NOA can be found on the website of the Jerusalem Institute of Justice: www.jij.org.il/ advocacy_sub.php?id=8

Chapter 8
Simon Azazian

S imon Azazian's father comes from an Armenian background. His mother is a Palestinian Christian.

Armenians have long been associated with Jerusalem. During the first century AD an Armenian battalion was stationed in Jerusalem and fought under the Roman emperor Titus. After Titus razed Jerusalem to the ground in AD 70 and expelled most of the Jews, the Romans imported Armenian merchants and administrators into the city.

The Apostles Bartholomew and Thaddeus visited Armenia in the first century AD and by 301 Armenia became the first nation to adopt Christianity as its official religion. Hence, the Armenian Orthodox Church is the oldest Christian community in the world.

Armenians have lived in Jerusalem for the past 1,700 years. The Armenian Quarter in the Old City was established in the fourteenth century and today there are approximately 2,500 Armenians living in Jerusalem, 500 of them within the Old City. There are a further 1,500 Armenians throughout Israel.

When the First World War ended and Palestine was liberated from the Ottoman Turks by the British, many

Armenian refugees moved into Jerusalem and settled in the Armenian Quarter in the Old City. These people had survived the Armenian Genocide, in which well over a million people died as a result of the deliberate and systematic destruction of the Armenian population of the Ottoman Empire, which started on 24 April 1915. It was on this day that Ottoman authorities arrested 250 Armenian intellectuals and leaders in society in Constantinople.

In the weeks and months that followed, the Ottoman military snatched Armenians from their homes and, deprived of food and water, they were forced to march for hundreds of miles into Syria. Needless to say, many people died on the way. Others survived, and this Armenian diaspora subsequently formed communities around the world. Many made their way to Jerusalem to join the existing Armenian community there.

Turkey, one of the countries that emerged from the Ottoman Empire, has always denied this genocide, which has left the Armenian people scattered around the world, feeling forgotten and without recompense.

For the 500 Armenians living in the Armenian Quarter of the Old City of Jerusalem today, where they occupy one-sixth of the space (the remainder being shared between the Jews, the Muslims and the Christians), the memories of their sad history linger. It is impossible to walk through this part of the Old City and not be reminded of the injustice this community has experienced. The Armenian Patriarchate owns most of the land here and this small, dwindling community, which keeps to itself, revolves around St James' Church, which dates from the twelfth century and is said to be the burial place of St James, the brother of Jesus.

It is against this backdrop that Simon Azazian's father was born. His grandfather came to Jerusalem after the

Armenian genocide; he walked all the way from Armenia to Syria, then on to Jordan before arriving in Jerusalem. Two generations later, Simon refers to himself as Armenian. Born in Jerusalem, he has spent most of his life there and now works there.

His mother is a Palestinian from a Greek Orthodox background, and her story is woven into the fabric of Simon's. Her father, Zuhdi Hashweh, grew up in Beersheva, where there was a large Palestinian Christian population at that time. However, Zuhdi's childhood was shattered when his father (Simon's great-grandfather) was taken by force to serve in the Turkish army and was never heard of again. Despite growing up in difficult circumstances, Zuhdi worked hard at school and went on to qualify as a lawyer. For over forty years he was the lawyer for the Greek Orthodox Patriarchate in Jerusalem and became a well-known and highly respected Jerusalemite.

You could be forgiven for thinking that any children born to a couple with such a sad history would be determined to find a comfortable and prosperous lifestyle in another region of the world. However, Simon's story is quite the reverse. He has deliberately decided to live in Jerusalem where, for the past ten years, he has been Director of Information and Public Relations for the Palestinian Bible Society, working to bring good news to the beleaguered Palestinian people living in the West Bank and at the same time forging links with Messianic Jewish believers in Israel.

Simon takes up his story.

During the first Palestinian Intifada (uprising), from 1987 to 1993, many Christians decided to leave the country because it was too hard living in an area of such conflict. Consequently, today, many Palestinian Christians have family all over the world, especially in the United States of America. Members of my dad's family were living in America, so, when I was a young boy, my parents decided to emigrate, and we lived in Los Angeles for two years.

However, it was quite tough; we had no sense of belonging and missed the unique community life that Arabs shared in Jerusalem. So, despite the ongoing conflict in Jerusalem, we decided to come back home and continue our lives here. It's amazing how God speaks to us during hard times. As Palestinian Christians we face many difficult situations on a day-to-day basis, because we are a minority amongst a minority; we find ourselves caught in a conflict we have no desire for! When we went to the States we thought we would have an easy life, but actually it wasn't, because there was no sense of belonging, and it was then that we started to search for something bigger.

I remember my mum watching Arab evangelists on television. In the early 1990s there were not many Arab evangelists on the Christian television channels – they were just beginning to emerge. It was at this time that God started to touch her heart, and she shared what she heard with us, and as a result I became a Christian when I was thirteen years old. I truly believe that when a seed is planted at a young age, even if it doesn't grow and develop from the start, it is still there, and the time will come for it to flourish. I think that is why today I have such a heart for people aged between twelve and fourteen, because if you can plant a seed of faith in their hearts and encourage them to believe in God for themselves, even if they drift away during their teenage years, the seed is there. I have seen many people who have come to the Lord after a number of years.

When we returned to Jerusalem in 1990, although the Intifada days of 1988 had cooled down, the remains of the struggle were evident all around us. I remember one afternoon. It was noontime and the streets were crowded as students left St George's School with excitement, trying to release the tension of the boring curriculum that had been taught in the school since the 1960s. As I was walking down Alzahra Street (a large commercial street in East Jerusalem) with four of my friends (who were all Muslims), it was like any other day and we were joking and laughing together.

Suddenly, as if from nowhere, as we were passing by, empty glass bottles and stones started to rain down on a small but new Israeli car that was parked near the Bible Society shop on the corner of Alzahra Street with Ibn Khaldon Street. The noise of glass shattering on the vehicle was closely followed by the sound of bullets being fired from M-16 rifles. We watched in alarm as Israeli soldiers came running towards us and we quickly realized we were caught in the middle of a very dangerous situation.

Staying close together, the four of us ran into the nearby alley of my grandfather's house that was hidden behind the busy streets. As we ran, none of us had the courage to look back over our shoulders. But we soon realized we had been joined by another young man wearing a black shirt with a *kofieh* (Arab headdress) covering his head. He started to limp, and I realized he was no longer keeping up with us. I shot a glance at him and saw him place his hand on his right leg, then fall to the ground. We had little time – the soldiers were not far behind us.

My mum looked anxious as she opened the door and

she placed her hands on my head, as if trying to grasp some of the fear out of my soul. Red-faced, hearts pounding, gasping for breath, we wiped the sweat off our young faces and were silent for a few seconds until Sami, one of my friends, let out a loud, scary scream and, placing his hand on his shirt, said, "My shirt... two holes... blood!" A bullet had gone through Sami's shirt, leaving two holes – one where it entered and the other where it went out. Lifting his shirt, we saw a dark-red scratch on his skin – the bullet had grazed his hip. Sami was OK. Today I look back and see God's hand of protection.

These and other experiences are engraved in my memory. When I was fifteen years old, I joined a summer "peace camp" which brought together young Israelis and Palestinians. This was a new thing, as the Peace Process was in its infancy. I had been a Christian for only two years, so I was a baby in the faith. I didn't know much and I was struggling with my own identity as well as the wider political struggle between our two peoples.

During this camp I shared a room with a nineteen-year-old Israeli guy called Udi. As I lay down to pray at night, Udi stopped me and asked, "What are you doing?"

I replied, "Praying."

He said, "Who to?"

"God," I replied.

"There is no such thing," retorted Udi.

As we quarrelled, I had little to offer by way of proof. I was new in my faith and it was hard for me to quote from the Bible.

"If God gives me one sign," said Udi, "then I will believe."

For two weeks, for the duration of that camp, I prayed every night for my enemy and friend.

"God, just give him one sign!" I prayed.

The two weeks passed and as I walked up to the bus to leave, I felt disappointed. I didn't dare say goodbye to Udi. But to my great surprise, he walked up to the bus and gave me a hug and whispered, "Simon, you were the sign from God!"

People ask me how I manage to carry God's heart for this region and care about both Palestinian people and Jewish people. When I became a true believer I learned that there is a big thing called "forgiveness". It can be hard to forget many things, especially when I pass an area of Jerusalem and I see a piece of land that used to belong to my grandfather. Or when I pass by my great-grandfather's house that was confiscated in 1967 and is now occupied by Jewish families, I am tempted to think how it could have been my house. But I have learned that whenever I have feelings of hatred in my heart and bad emotions start to come back, I take them to the cross. It is there I take all my emotions and all my worries, and I simply ask God to work in my heart. I remind myself that there are always two sides to the coin. Israel has a wonderful humanitarian side. I saw it recently when my colleagues were under persecution in Gaza, and Israel allowed the whole team to leave there and come to Bethlehem. So I have learned not to judge or condemn. Rather, I leave these matters to God and ask Him to help me share His love.

I am a Palestinian Arab Christian living in Jerusalem, yet I enjoy close fellowship with Messianic Jewish believers. This can only happen because we look at each other as brothers and sisters, regardless of our background. I truly believe that as a Palestinian Christian, I have the complete freedom to be in fellowship with Messianic believers – indeed, believers from any background – because we are all children of God. I believe that this in itself is a clear example of the peace that can only be reached through Jesus Christ. There are no other solutions. The Peace Process and other ideas proposed by various governments around the world will all fail, because true peace can only be found in Christ. This message is very important and very strong.

If you ask me what I believe God is doing here in Israel and the Palestinian Areas today, I have to reply that I believe God is doing quite a lot! We don't always see what He is doing because He is working at a spiritual level. However, on a day-to-day basis, when you live in Jerusalem you start seeing things and you start understanding how God is moving amongst the people. Many are seeing visions. Others are having dreams. They are coming to the Lord. Many people come to Jerusalem to see the historical sites, but when they meet the "living stones", the local believers, their lives are touched to see there are people here who carry the love and the passion of Christ. So I believe that God is doing a great work, despite all the bad news that we constantly hear.

We organize teams to play basketball every Friday, and one day a young Palestinian guy approached me because he knew I was a Christian and asked if we could talk privately together. He was quite shy, so we moved to one side and he told me that he had had a vision of Christ. "I dreamt of Jesus Christ," he said. "He came to me and He took me to the Old City walls. He told me to sit down near the Damascus Gate, where He took out a Bible, and He told me to start reading the Bible. But Simon," he said, "I don't have a Bible."

A week later I sneaked a Bible into his backpack and he

started to read it. A couple of weeks later he asked me a direct question: "Is Jesus the Lord?"

I told him, "Yes."

But I could see it was hard for him to believe this. So we prayed that he would have another dream, and that same night, Jesus came to him and said, "I am your Lord."

The next question he asked me was, "Am I the only one?" He really thought he was the only person with a Muslim background who had experienced dreams about Jesus. I told him there are many other people who are having these visions who are meeting together. I subsequently introduced him to one of these groups and also to a church, where now they are following up and taking good care of him.

For somebody from a Muslim background, to become a Christian is an enormous step to take. According to the Muslim religion, if you stop being a Muslim, after three days they have the right to kill you. So that is the difficulty. In Islam you cannot change your religion. I have heard so many stories of people being kicked out of their houses for challenging the Muslim faith. Others we have lost contact with – we don't know what has happened to them. We don't know whether they are with the Lord or where they are.

So it is a challenge for a Muslim to become a Christian. And when they do take that step, further problems emerge when they want to find a wife. Do you choose a Muslim wife or do you choose a Christian wife? If you choose a wife from a Christian background, her family will not easily welcome you because, when they take one look at your background, they may not accept that you have become a believer in Christ, because to them you are still a Muslim with a Muslim name.

And even if you do eventually find a Christian wife and marry her, what about the children? What school are you going to send them to? Because of your Muslim name, on their identity card it will be written that they are Muslim, so they will be required to have a Muslim education. I know cases of Christian couples from Muslim backgrounds who are suffering with their children because whenever they visit their (Muslim) grandparents, the children come back home and start putting down their prayer mats to pray to Allah. So it's not easy.

Palestinians who are brought up in a Muslim community are intrinsically involved with Muslim culture; it is impossible to separate the two. For example, during Ramadan, when Muslims fast all day, a person who has become a Christian finds himself involved in this dilemma – what should he do? Many tell me they fast for Christ; they have to find a way of dealing with these problems.

We at the Palestinian Bible Society are very involved in our society and we believe that our mandate is "To live and give, to serve and proclaim the Word of God." I believe that we are a living testimony to the Word of God. Our lives are like a "fifth gospel" – we are the only gospel that people will ever "read". People are hungry and it's hard to give them a Bible when what they want is a loaf of bread. I believe that we should give a person a Bible whenever we have the opportunity. We proclaim the Word of God through the media and through the newspapers whenever we have the opportunity, and we know it brings a lot of comfort and it brings a different message to the message the people are used to hearing here. We talk about loving your enemy, turning the other cheek, and walking the extra mile. These things are new and unique to the suffering community.

Both during and after the war between Hamas, in Gaza, and Israel during the winter of 2008–2009, we have been able to help over 4,000 Muslim families in Gaza with relief packages. And recently we started a water-filtering project for people there because the water can be so polluted and sick people, especially those who have kidney disease, need to have clean water. So in cooperation with Christians all over the world, we have been able to install water filters inside many houses. We organize activities for children and always bring a message of love and hope to them. We help those who are sick and needy, and we work in the schools – just to show the people love. In the end, I believe Christianity is a lifestyle – it is not a religion that you impose on people. It's a simple message that says, "God is love."

Chapter 9
Yoyakim Figueras

Like most of the people who find themselves leading churches or congregations in Israel today, Yoyakim Figueras has an unusual story. Yet it would seem that this uniqueness, this individuality, is what gives people like Yoyakim the ability to cope with extremely unpleasant and challenging circumstances.

Yoyakim's parents met in Israel. His mother is Dutch and his father is Spanish. Both his parents have remarkable stories of their own. That they should meet and marry, become Israeli citizens and raise five sons there is quite a story in itself.

But for Yoyakim that was just the beginning, perhaps the preparation, for what lay ahead. He served in the Israeli Defence Force (IDF) and still is a reservist. He went on to university and qualified as a social worker. Along with his wife Debbie, who is Jewish, and their family (they now have six young children), they settled in Arad, which is situated in the south of Israel in the Negev, and Yoyakim worked in a school in nearby Beersheva for disadvantaged children.

In this chapter, Yoyakim describes what happened next and how his expectations of life rapidly changed as he

found himself forced into years of confrontation that were not of his choosing.

My parents met in Israel. My mother is Dutch. My father is Catalan Spanish from a Catholic background. He was actually a Catholic monk in a monastery high up in the jagged Montserrat mountains near the city of Barcelona in Catalonia, Spain. After some years there, he left the monastery and made his way to Israel. And here in Israel he met my mother. From a Dutch Reformed background, my mother's family were enthusiastic Zionists. During the Second World War they hid a Jewish friend, a lady called Mrs Bunning whose husband used to work with my grandfather. When Mr Bunning was arrested by the Nazis and taken to Auschwitz, my mother's parents (my grandparents) risked everything to hide his wife. Her husband died in Auschwitz, so after the war Mrs Bunning stayed with the family and my mother grew up always knowing her.

I later found out that my mother tried to persuade Mrs Bunning to travel with her to Israel. "It's your land," my mother told her, "you should go there."

"No," she had replied, "the only friends I have are here in Holland."

Both my parents received Israeli citizenship, which is unusual for non-Jewish people. The amazing thing is, the day after Mrs Bunning died, my mother received her Israeli citizenship. She felt it was as though God was saying to her, "It was the old woman's place to be here in the Land, but I am giving it to you instead."

So along with my four brothers, we all grew up here in Israel as Israelis although we were not Jewish. We were raised to believe in Jesus and the Bible (both the Old and New Testament), and spoke Hebrew as our main language. Like every Israeli citizen, I did my army service. Then I studied social work and now, several years later, I am the pastor of a small congregation in Arad where we have Jews and Gentiles together.

Over the years people from a wide variety of backgrounds have joined the congregation. We have an Arab lady from a Muslim background who came to faith in Jesus. We have had people from an ultra-Orthodox background come to faith; they were with us for a while before moving on to another place. We have new immigrants and Sabras (native-born Israelis). It's quite a mix! Every *Shabbat* (Sabbath) we average about forty people and we always have translations into a number of languages including English, Spanish, Arabic and Russian.

Growing up, I always felt Israeli. I was Israeli. I wasn't a Dutch citizen and I wasn't a Spanish citizen. My parents, when they became Israeli citizens, had to give up their previous nationalities and hand in their passports. My parents did not speak Dutch or Spanish to each other, rather they spoke Hebrew. I was always aware of the fact that I was not Jewish and people around me were aware of that. But it didn't make any difference – I was an Israeli citizen. From time to time our parents were worried about our identity and sometimes talked about moving to Holland or Canada. But I was one of those who insisted on staying in Israel.

My wife, Debbie, is Jewish. She was born in Nahariya (a town in northern Israel, close to the border with Lebanon). Her mother is a Jew from London and her father was a Jew with an Iraqi background. Like so many Jewish people, his family moved from place to place. He was born in Japan to an Iraqi Jewish businessman. He then grew up in India and Egypt, but just after the State of Israel was established in 1948, the Iraqis notified him that his Iraqi citizenship had been cancelled. So the British gave him a British passport and in England he met my mother-in-law, Ruth, and together they made *aliyah* (emigrated) to Israel.

Debbie and I moved from Beersheva to Arad at the end of 1998 and we now have six children. Arad is a city of 25,000 people and within the population there is a growing minority (currently around 2,000 people) of a particular group of ultra-Orthodox Jews called the Ger Hasidic sect. This particular branch of Judaism originated in Poland, taking its name from the town of Gora Kalwaria (pronounced "Calvaria") in the Warsaw district.

When we moved to Arad, I was still working full time as a social worker in Beersheva. After a few weeks of living here, it became obvious that we should start a small Bible study in our house. So once a week on a Tuesday night we met with two or three other believers. The group expanded and the congregation we have today is the result. When we first moved to Arad we were still members of Nachalat Yeshua (Yeshua's Inheritance), the congregation in Beersheva where Howard Bass is the pastor, but after a while we all realized we should be holding a *Shabbat* service in Arad and be independent.

However, shortly before we moved to Arad something very significant happened that was to change the course of my professional life. In November 1998 there was a pogrom against the Beersheva congregation when about a thousand angry ultra-Orthodox men surrounded the building, and the police were called to help us escape. I was targeted by these religious Jews as being a social worker in charge of a group of children at a boarding-school, and the chief rabbi of Beersheva started to make life difficult for me. He called my boss to his office and warned him that a "missionary" was working at the school. He said, "We have pictures of him taking children to the monastery" (that was what he called the Beersheva congregation).

Of course, this was not true. I was always careful to make sure I did not mix my faith with my work, because the school was government funded and I knew that I was not allowed to mention my faith there. The staff knew what I believed; but the children had no idea that I was anything other than a social worker. I always found it sad that I was not allowed to share my faith with them, because they were children from very disturbed backgrounds and it was frustrating for me, believing I had an answer for them and not being able to share it.

All this happened at the time we moved to Arad. We did not move because of this trouble; rather, events just coincided. I resigned from my job as a social worker at the school in Beersheva and decided to take some time out to consider our future, realizing that if I was to become busy with believers in a congregation, I could not also be working in a place where I could not share my faith. I also realized I would continue to be targeted by the ultra-Orthodox, who could accuse me of working with "weak" people and taking advantage of them. It was true that I was caring for weak people, but I never took advantage of my position.

And so for the next six months I worked on a construction site before beginning studies at the Israel College of the Bible in preparation for working full time with the congregation.

The experience of being under attack from the ultra-religious Jews in Beersheva was a foretaste of what was to come. Since starting the congregation in Arad we have experienced ongoing harassment from the ultra-Orthodox, and it is challenging. They frequently demonstrate outside our house and make a lot of noise. They harass me and my wife and our children. They stand with signs in front of our house, shouting that we are dangerous people and enemies of the Jewish people. They curse us and mock us and laugh at us. So what should our reaction be? On one occasion I was pushing one of our children in the pram, a little baby who was sound asleep, and one of these guys purposefully put his foot in front of the pram, jolting it to a stop. The baby woke up. Nobody was hurt, but how did that make me feel towards that person? I have to be honest and admit that it brings out the most negative feelings towards them. However, I also know that Jesus teaches us to turn the other cheek and to love our enemies.

During one of these demonstrations I felt particularly angry towards these people and when I caught myself thinking those thoughts, I started to praise God. Praising God changed me and I was able to love them, despite what they were doing outside our house. It's not easy and it brings an awareness that the struggle is between the flesh and the spirit.

Now, years later and still enduring this abusive behaviour, we are very aware of the nature of the battle, and as a congregation we have learned to pray for others much more. We pray continually for those ultra-Orthodox people. We understand where their anger is coming from because history has shown that Christians have done much damage to the Jews and made it very difficult for them to accept Jesus as their Messiah. But it goes back even beyond the 2,000 years of history between the church and the Jewish people, because Jesus Himself was persecuted by the religious Jews of His day. They hated Him.

We are very aware that we are involved in an intense spiritual battle and that the people coming against us are actually in bondage. They are in the bondage of hatred. They are blinded. With this awareness, we pray for them and we are trying not to be a stumbling-block for them. When they eventually accept Yeshua as their Messiah, I don't want them to say to me, "You were such a stumbling-block for me." I would like them to say, "We were so jealous of you. We really wanted to have what you have." So that's what it did to me and to us as a congregation.

We understand we are at a very critical time in history. Even though we are facing hardships in Arad, I do not call it persecution. Compared to what Christians in other parts of the world have to endure, we may be going through challenging times, but we still have freedom to practise our faith. However, I believe this time of freedom may not last much longer – I believe time is short and we believers need to prepare for more difficult times ahead, both in Israel and in other places around the world. I also believe Israel is going to face very hard opposition from the countries around it and also from the wider world. Jerusalem is a stumbling-block, as Zechariah said.

We are trying to teach our children that even more difficult times are coming and that when they grow up, they will most likely have to face much harder persecution. We are teaching them how to hold on to the Lord and be ready for when these times come, and to be ready for His coming.

Israel is like the clock of God's Word. For almost 2,000 years it seemed as though God was not concerned with Israel and the physical Jewish nation. Many thought that the church had taken the spiritual place of Israel and the physical nation of Israel no longer had any part in God's plan. But since Israel was established in 1948 it has become clear to many Gentile Christians that God does have a plan for Israel. If you read the books of the prophets in the Old Testament, it is very hard not to understand that God has fulfilled and is fulfilling prophecies today and that Jesus is coming back to this land of Israel, as we read in Acts chapter 1. We also read in Zechariah that the Jewish people, the Israelites, will see Him; that when He returns, the nation of Israel will see the "one they have pierced" (Zechariah 12:10). So therefore, just as it is clear that the Jewish people coming from the nations of the world to live in the land of Israel (and they are continuing to return here) is a fulfilment of prophecy, then it is also clear that all the prophecies that say, "I will be their God and they will be my people" will happen. As Paul says in Romans 11, when God restores Israel and reveals Himself to the Jewish people, it will be like "life from the dead" (Romans 11:15).

These are biblical prophecies, and the Christian world, the true believers in Jesus, must recognize and acknowledge that God is doing something great, something that history has been waiting for a long time to happen.

Israel is not yet a believing nation. The majority of Israelis are secularists and do not believe in God at all. And many religious Jews, those who claim to believe in God, refuse to recognize Jesus as Messiah. As Christians we should be praying much for the Jewish people, because the fact that Jewish people are back in the land is a sign that our Lord is coming back to His people as well as to all of us Christians all over the world.

Recently we have been encouraged because one of the Orthodox group who have been demonstrating outside our house for years came to me and said, "Yoyakim, I want to talk to you." I thought he was going to say something very rude to me but instead he said, "I want to apologize for everything I did in coming against you and your family. I understand you are a human being and your family are human beings. Please forgive me." To me, this is an encouraging sign that something is happening.

When I look beyond Israel's borders to what is happening in the Arab world, I see the oppression that the Arab nations are experiencing from their own governments. But the question is, what will happen next? There is a fear that Islamic powers will take over. We saw this happen in the Gaza Strip when Israel withdrew from there. The Palestinians held elections and Hamas won. Hamas is an extreme fundamentalist Islamic party that applies Shariah law and is intolerant of any other religion. There was a small Christian community in Gaza, and an even smaller Evangelical community there. One of their number was kidnapped by Islamists and murdered. There is therefore a fear that these powers will take over in the rest of the Arab world. If that is the case, then it's not very promising.

But recently, in Jerusalem, I met a former Shi'ite Muslim from Iran. Today he is a Christian and he told me that there are over a million Christians in Iran, and the numbers are growing. These people are tired of Islam and are finding fresh hope in Jesus.

Chapter 10
"C", an Arab Christian

Whilst many Christians do follow events in Israel closely, it is perhaps true to say that most have little or no idea of what life is like in the Palestinian Areas of Israel (known as the West Bank) for the tiny minority of Palestinian Christians who live there – Christians who come from a Muslim background. Recently I received an apologetic email from a lady in America who, after reading an article I had written about a Palestinian Christian living in East Jerusalem, wrote to admit she had not realized there were any Palestinians who were Christians, because she had wrongly assumed that all Palestinians are Islamist extremists intent on the destruction of the Jewish people and the State of Israel!

This story provides us with an insight into what life is like for Evangelical Arab/Palestinian Christians living in Israel and the West Bank who feel compelled to share their faith in Jesus with their Arab/Palestinian Muslim neighbours.

At this point it may be helpful to clarify who is referred to as an Arab and who is a Palestinian. Identity is a crucial subject in Israel and the West Bank! At its simplest, Arabs living within Israel are referred to as Israeli Arabs whilst Arabs living in the West Bank are referred to as Palestinians (because they live under the auspices of the Palestinian Authority rather than the Israeli Government). So, Jewish people live in Israel only (they are not allowed to travel into areas of the West Bank that are under Palestinian control), whilst Arab people live in both Israel (Israeli Arabs) and the West Bank (Palestinians). However, whilst an Israeli Arab can travel in and out of the West Bank, a Palestinian cannot leave the West Bank unless he has a special permit. It is these people who find themselves living like pawns in the political game that is being played around them, and as a consequence they believe their situation to be hopeless.

Arab people (both Israeli Arabs and Palestinians) are identified as being either Christian or Muslim. Of the minority of Israeli Arabs who describe themselves as Christian, a significant number come from an Orthodox background (usually Greek Orthodox). In recent years, some of these people have left the Greek Orthodox Church to join the growing number of Evangelical Arab Christian churches. This has resulted in tension between the Orthodox Church and Evangelical Christians. Hence Evangelical Arab Christians find themselves a minority group within the Christian minority. There are growing numbers of Evangelical Arab churches in Israel, most notably in Haifa, Nazareth and Jerusalem.

The majority of Israeli Arabs are Muslims and live in towns and villages mainly in the north of Israel, as well as in East Jerusalem. Compared to Palestinians living in the West Bank, life is good for Israeli Arabs. They have their own democratically elected politicians (Members of Knesset) within the Israeli Government and share the same

114

benefits as Israeli Jews (although they are not obliged to serve in the army). Many Israeli Arabs are highly qualified, having gained excellent degrees in Israeli universities. Few would change places with their brothers living in the West Bank, where conditions under the Palestinian Authority are very different.

So why does this story have to be anonymous? Quite simply because this is a matter of life and death. If a Muslim Palestinian person living in the West Bank changes his faith and chooses to become a Christian, he or she faces expulsion from their family and possibly even death. It is a shameful and forbidden thing for a Muslim to renounce Islam. To then embrace the God of Israel and His Son Jesus Christ, the Messiah, is unthinkable. But despite the dangers, it is happening. And it is happening for two reasons.

The first reason is supernatural: there are many reports coming out of the West Bank of Muslims having dreams and visions of Jesus, and as a result coming to faith in Him. Many remain secret believers, for fear of their lives. The second reason is that a small but significant number of Arab/Palestinian Christians are going into the towns and villages of the West Bank, where the population is entirely Muslim, and courageously sharing the gospel message about Jesus. They are doing this quietly and cautiously, never knowing whether the person they are talking to is likely to report their presence in the area and thereby endanger their life.

This chapter is based on the story of one Evangelical Arab Christian – let's call him "C" – and his wife, who believe that there is about to be a "tidal wave" of Muslims becoming Christians from the Arab nations of the world, including the West Bank in Israel, and that the church needs to prepare for huge numbers of new believers.

C is brave. Like many Arab Christians, he has his own business. But he is spending less and less time there because now he believes the time has come for him to respond to a vision he had a few years ago. At first this vision shocked him when he realized that God wanted him, along with his wife, to concentrate their efforts on sharing their faith and the gospel message about Jesus with the majority of the Palestinian people (who are Muslim) who live in the West Bank.

I met C recently and he shared his story.

I never really thought about the West Bank when I was first saved. But then, in 2004, I was praying with my wife when we both saw the same vision. We saw a large "room" surrounded by four tall walls. The room had no ceiling – it looked like a huge courtyard. Positioned in one of the walls was a big gate that was closed. It looked just like one of the gates in the Old City of Jerusalem. We saw a large crowd of people and they were banging on the gate, wanting it to open so they could escape. At the same time I saw many tall cranes lifting crates of food and supplies from outside the wall to the people in the "room". I recognized some believers that I knew speaking to the people through the gate.

As we talked together about this vision, my wife and I both had the impression that somehow, somebody had to open the gate, and we felt God was calling us to do that. We realized at the same time that this would not be an easy job; rather, whoever did this would be crushed by the multitudes of people behind those walls.

And that was when we started to prepare ourselves for going to the West Bank. Until this happened, I was sure the main area God had wanted me to engage with was in building strong relationships with some Messianic Jewish believers I had met when I first became a Christian some years earlier. For many years we have been meeting to study the Bible and pray together. We discuss our differences in a spirit of reconciliation and trust, and this has helped all of us to better understand the other person's point of view, whilst at the same time realizing that God wants us to be one in mind and spirit.

So when my wife and I had this vision, at first I was confused because when I became a Christian, I immediately recognized the importance of reconciliation between Jewish and Arab believers, yet this vision seemed different to what was originally on my heart. For years I had been praying regularly with Jewish believers and asking the Lord to unite us more and more. So now I began to pray that the Lord would help me understand more fully what He was asking us to do next.

One morning, a little while later, I was praying on Mount Zion when a picture came into my mind. I saw a puzzle with five pieces and someone was trying to join the pieces together; but no matter how hard he tried, the pieces would not fit. I didn't understand what this meant so I asked the Lord to show me. I remembered the earlier vision of the crowd banging on the gate and realized how difficult it would be to unite all those people into one body – it would be an impossible thing to put together, just like the puzzle that had only five pieces. Then I understood that the Lord was showing me something that would be even more challenging to achieve – how to unite all those Muslim people (who knew nothing about Jesus, let alone the church) with the existing church structure.

Here in Israel and especially in the West Bank, Muslim

Background Believers (MBBs) are treated with suspicion when they try to join an existing church where the people have come from a Christian Arab background. I know the problem well. At the same time, my spirit was excited because the Lord was giving me a glimpse of a future time, maybe in the near future, when large numbers of Muslim people would come running into the Kingdom of God, and we, the existing Christians, had to be ready to receive and welcome them.

When we started going into the West Bank we quickly realized the Palestinian people are desperate for the Lord. I am not exaggerating when I say that 50 per cent of the people we meet, when they find out we are Christian, will start speaking to us about God. Half of those will want to proselytize to us about Islam but the other half will want to know about Christ. So 25 per cent of the population are really very interested to know about Christ, and that is very encouraging and represents a lot of people! However, those 25 per cent, even when they know the truth, are not always willing to take that step of faith because it is really dangerous for them. It is dangerous both on a religious level and on a cultural level involving traditions and family.

However, despite the dangers, there are now a significant number of believers in the West Bank. They need our help and our prayers. I know that the land of Israel is a key place at this time because it is the place that is going to open up the final release of God's work in the last days of human history.

I asked C to describe some of the people he is in touch with in the West Bank. Obviously he was not able to name names, because as already mentioned, this is far too sensitive and dangerous at this present time.

It began with our relief work amongst the believers, which is necessary because the Palestinian Christians we are talking about are amongst the poorest in that society. However, to be frank, the situation of the Palestinian people is not as poor as Africa, for example. We have to put things into perspective. If a Palestinian were to hear me saying this, he may be upset. But really, when you go there, even those with low-paid jobs have a satellite dish and a colour television, whereas in Africa you can travel from village to village and see that they have no electricity or running water.

But even so, the financial situation is not easy in the West Bank because the average monthly salary is 1,200 Israeli shekels (equivalent to 300–400 US dollars), and in many areas of life prices are at exactly the same high level as in Israel. So the rich are getting richer whilst the poor are getting even poorer. It is impossible to take good care of your family there. If you don't own your own house and if you are not living in a village, where things are a little bit cheaper, there is almost no way you can break out of the poverty trap. The economy is weak. Despite the support they receive, there is little or no industry and the Palestinian Authority is currently not actively planning to encourage agriculture or industry.

Politically, I do not see any solution for the Palestinian people or for any of the surrounding Arab nations. I see the storms that are happening in many Arab countries and I can see that in the near future, it may happen in the West Bank as well. Maybe within months, there will be a big revolt against the Palestinian Authority, especially by the youth. Democracy is a culture, it is not a political system. It has to grow from within and there are no short cuts – it takes time. So it will probably take two generations before today's youth have their dreams fulfilled, and because progress will be slow, there will be a growing desperation in the Arab world.

I also believe there will be another wave of revolution that will engulf Saudi Arabia and Iran, and this will result in a wave of salvation. However, what concerns me at this present time is that I don't see the church prepared to receive these people. We pray for revival but we are not prepared for it.

So for us Arabs from a Christian background, the challenge is to prepare ourselves to open our hearts to the Muslim people. And that is a challenge. With all the trouble of the past years, we have turned in on ourselves and closed our minds to these people. My prayer is that the Lord will give us a sense of urgency and a feeling that Jesus' return is near and we have to be prepared.

Also in this land I pray that we will open our hearts. I have found that many Arab Christians, when they open their hearts to the Muslim people, automatically open their hearts to Jewish people too. Throughout history, we have closed our hearts to both peoples – Isaac and Ishmael. We rejected the Jewish people and also we isolated ourselves from the Muslims. So I believe our calling as Christian Arabs in the Arab world is to embrace both. And that is a very unique calling. Please pray for us that we assume this position and do what the Lord wants us to do at this time in history.

Christians in the West will be reading this story whilst C is in the Middle East living out his Christian life in difficult and challenging circumstances. As he said, working amongst Muslims is dangerous work; it could cost C his life. So I asked him how the church in the West could help in this work. His answer may surprise you.

To be honest, when I look at the church in the West, in my opinion, it is even sadder than our situation here. I do not look to the Western Christians as the ones who are going to bring us help. Rather, I think we are the people who are going to help them.

I really do think that the church in the West has a wrong perspective about Islam. Our main problem is the devil. The devil uses secularism, socialism, Islam, "false" Christianity – and he uses the opportunity of any situation in which the current system or culture seems to be failing to offer the temptation of a "replacement" system. So Islam is not our enemy. The devil is our enemy. We really have to focus on the revival of the church and preparedness, because that is the key issue; that is what will change history.

God wants to use the church and I hope there will be an awakening in the church in the West. That is the best thing they could do for us! I am grateful for the faithful remnant who pray for us and support us; I know that it is not easy for the church in Europe. But still my message to them is that we need to work together, to cooperate and prepare for the wave of new believers from the Muslim world – it is near. Storms are happening in the Arab nations.

We have learned two biblical principles. The first is that God always wants the best for any nation. The second is that He knows what is best for any nation. So with everything that is happening around us, His will is for salvation to come to the people – we have to be sure about that.

Chapter 11
Etti Shoshani

I first met Etti Shoshani in Jerusalem at Ramat Rachel, a hotel which is situated to the south of the city and which overlooks Bethlehem and the security wall that now surrounds much of the West Bank.

We decided the coffee shop would be a good place to talk and found a table outside on the veranda overlooking the ancient biblical town of Bethlehem, nestled as it is between the folds of the hills that once would have been the site of the fields where the shepherds tended their flocks. It is almost a surreal experience, standing in Israel and looking across the border line into the West Bank, much of which is now run by the Palestinian Authority. It is another world. A world that is only five miles down the road, where they speak a different language and where the majority of the population are Muslim people. From this vantage point you become acutely aware of just how challenging it is to meet those on the "other side" and fully understand their cultural, theological and political views. Etti's story, as it unfolds, demonstrates this perfectly.

Etti is Jewish and a believer in Jesus – or Yeshua, to use His Hebrew name. Etti told me that she was born in Israel. Her father, who was also born there, came from a very religious family, but "he rebelled against Judaism as a young man." Her mother, on the other hand, although from a less strictly religious background, was the one who kept the Jewish traditions alive in the family when Etti was growing up.

"We kept the feasts," Etti told me, "and we talked a little bit about God. We were also taught the biblical principles of purity and behaviour."

She told me how, from a young age, she had struggled with her fear of dying, her quest for the meaning of life and her questions about life after death. After finishing her studies at university and after her father's death, she left Israel for several months to travel across Europe, as most Israelis do after their army service. While travelling, she was hoping to find the answers to life that she so longed for.

Her life was to change forever when, in 1979, at the age of 26, she became a believer in Yeshua the Messiah. Etti now tells her story of how that happened.

I somehow knew that when I left Israel and went to Europe, I would find the answer. But when I found the answer, I didn't fully understand it. The problem was that I heard some wonderful testimonies from believers, but they didn't fully understand the importance of showing a Jew like me the scriptures to support their claims that only Yeshua could totally change the life of a sinner.

In order for me to feel confident about believing that Yeshua really was the Messiah, I had to understand the prophecies in the Old Testament. So I started to study the Bible when I returned to Israel. Beginning in Genesis chapter 1, I read through the whole Old Testament, and then it became clear to me that Yeshua had fulfilled every prophecy concerning His first coming as Messiah. I saw that the timing and the place of His birth were fulfilled accurately. When I eventually understood that He alone was the atonement for our sin and that it was not possible to receive forgiveness any other way, I realized I had found what I was looking for.

The believers I knew at that time were the people who had helped me to study the Old Testament. Some of them were Jewish believers and some were Gentile believers. I had been watching their lives closely and they were such an example to me of how to trust God and how to effectively pray – both of which had not been a part of my life. I was also deeply touched by the love and respect they had for one another, things which are not so common in Israeli society.

I gave careful thought to the personal implications of becoming a believer in Jesus, knowing the likely reaction from my family, my friends and the Israeli people as a whole. I realized the cost could involve rejection from my family, the loss of my friends and even persecution. After I accepted Yeshua as my Messiah and Lord, it wasn't long before I lost most of my friends.

During our conversation Etti often looked into the distance beyond the security wall into Bethlehem and the West Bank, a place where Jewish people are now forbidden to go. There was once a time when she could have driven the short distance to Bethlehem without worrying about her personal security. Many Jewish people used to enjoy meeting friends and visiting the restaurants there. Rachel's tomb lies at the entrance to the town. It is a place that holds great significance for both Jewish and Christian people.

But today, sadly, all that has changed and it has become off limits for Jewish people due to security reasons. Etti continued:

Twenty months later, my younger brother came to faith in Yeshua, and that led to our rejection by most of my father's family. It was also the time when my twin brother heard about me and my younger brother coming to faith in Yeshua. He became very angry with us and even today, our relationship is quite cool. That is part of counting the cost before coming to faith.

I asked Etti what she did when she came to faith.

I joined the fellowship at Beit Immanuel (Emmanuel House) in Jaffa, one of the earliest Messianic congregations in modern Israel. Over the years the numbers grew rapidly and it was there that I was properly nurtured and discipled.

The vision of Beit Immanuel was to disciple faithful men and women, within the context of the local congregation, who would in turn impart to others the values and disciplines of a faithful Messianic lifestyle. Later I joined the staff of the congregation and worked in the hostel which was situated in the same grounds.

Many Jewish people were becoming believers in Yeshua at the end of the 1970s and the beginning of the 1980s. It was truly a move of God and it was very exciting. We all had to face some great challenges and hardships. We also had to find our way in Israeli society, understand the Jewish roots of our faith and learn how to relate to our Gentile brothers and sisters who poured their lives into ours. We were all going through a tremendous time of growth, change and adaptation.

Today, many years later, Etti is a Bible teacher and she is also participating in the women's activities of a Christian organization called Musalaha (an Arabic word meaning "reconciliation").

For the past fifteen years I have been teaching the Word of God and giving people the "tools" necessary to study the Bible. I believe this is so important, because when you learn how to study the Word of God for yourself, you have the tools to discover the truth which is life-changing. This is vital for all believers because it equips us for Godly life in general and for the days that lie ahead in particular. The method I use is very simple and systematic. It is called the Inductive Bible Study Method, which uses the Word of God as the primary source. You mark the Word. You make some lists. When you discover the facts for yourself, then you understand how to correctly interpret what you read within the context of the chapter or passage you are studying. Then you can implement what you have learned into your daily walk with the Lord. It's a great method for studying and implementing the Word of God.

I have two passions. My first is for truth. My second is to teach and equip the body of believers here in the land. Why? Because in these chaotic days it is easy to look for some quick, easy solution rather than let the Holy Spirit, through the Word, guide, transform and renew your mind. The best way to avoid living a lukewarm spiritual life and being deceived is to intimately know the Word of God.

I was interested to know why, as a Jewish believer, Etti is involved with an organization (Musalaha) working towards reconciliation with Palestinian Christians.

For many years I had known some of the facts about what Israel had been doing to and with the Palestinians, but I had always believed my country was right. Finally, in 2005, when I was asked to participate in a women's conference of Musalaha, I did it with fear and trembling because I didn't really know how to relate to my Palestinian sisters in the faith. However, when I met them I found out that they were as normal as I was! They also didn't know how to relate to Jews or what to expect of us. As we got to know one another we were able to hear what life was like from the "other side", and what I heard broke my heart.

I decided I needed to undertake some research and find out more for myself about what was really going on. I realized that what we hear today from the secular media is often distorted and biased towards one side or the other.

As sisters in the Lord, I believe we have to allow Christ to be the common ground for us, and from that position try to encourage each other and see what we have in common and what we can do together. From experience, I now understand that we can do a lot when we learn to accept each other. We are learning how to pray for each other and how to identify with each other's pain and suffering. As we gradually draw closer to each other, we are experiencing what it means to be joined together as members of the body of Christ. When Jewish and Palestinian believers unite at this deep level, it is an amazing experience for us all, and hopefully a powerful testimony in our communities.

I put it to Etti that in the West, it is very common for Christians to take sides, either in favour of Israel and against the Palestinians, or vice versa.

I do not believe we should take sides. I believe the only side we can take is for the Messiah and for the truth of the Word of God. There are many sensitive issues that are difficult for us to agree on and understand, especially issues to do with the land of Israel. But as long as we do not allow those differences to prevent us from agreeing on the main tenets of the Word of God, I do not see why we cannot work together. I do not believe we are to take sides; if we do, we will run into problems.

One of the questions asked in *The Olive Tree* radio series is "What is God doing in Israel and the Palestinian Areas today?" So I asked Etti for her comment on this.

I would say that in Israel, because we have such a spiritual, ideological and political vacuum, many are searching for the truth, especially the young generation, which is very open to all things spiritual. We are finding today that when these young people come to know the Lord, they have such a boldness and eagerness to share the truth and share their testimonies in order to challenge the way our society lives and what it believes about Yeshua. They do not have the fear and caution that many of us, who are now in our forties and fifties, used to have about sharing our faith. They are more confident and are finding their way in society better than we did at their age. The young people of today will be our evangelists, teachers and leaders of tomorrow. Indeed, many of them are already functioning in these roles. I also believe the generation that is now emerging from the army and who realize first-hand what is going on, is more open to reconciliation. They are hearing for themselves what the Palestinian brothers and sisters have to suffer.

Concerning what I believe God is doing in the West Bank, the churches are growing and many Muslims are coming to faith. This involves serious persecution for both believers from a Muslim background and Christian Arabs who try to help them.

I asked Etti what it means to her to pray for the peace of Jerusalem, as we are exhorted to do in the Psalms.

It simply means to pray for the coming of the Lord, because He is the only answer for all the complicated situations we are facing here in the Middle East. The Bible teaches us that only Yeshua Himself can change the hearts of men to do things God's way.

Chapter 12
Sabha Asmar

ew programmes in *The Olive Tree* radio series have provoked as much response as the interview with Sabha Asmar. A single lady now approaching old age, Sabha is blind and lives alone in a humble one-roomed dwelling in a suburb of Bethlehem. I was introduced to her by Paul Calvert, a young Christian from England who works as a broadcast journalist in the town. He met Sabha through the pastor of St Paul's Church in Jerusalem.

Sabha used to be able to travel into Jerusalem and she attended St Paul's Church. However, permission for Palestinians to travel from Bethlehem into Israel stopped some time ago. The pastor of the church was nervous about travelling into the West Bank, and as Paul frequently travelled between Bethlehem and Jerusalem, he was asked to visit Sabha – something he has continued doing for some years now.

The day we visited Sabha, I drove with Paul from Jerusalem to Bethlehem, a journey of only five miles. These days, there is a checkpoint to cross – nobody goes in or out of Bethlehem without being checked by both Israeli and Palestinian security soldiers; foreigners need to show their passports and locals need the correct ID and pass to move between Israel and the West Bank. No Jewish person is allowed into Bethlehem – the Palestinian Authority cannot guarantee their safety.

The checkpoint is an intimidating and grim place. It looks ugly and feels hostile. Nobody likes it. The queues can be long. The wait is frustrating. But that is the reality of life here.

Eventually we were through to the other side and began our drive along the streets of Bethlehem to the suburb where Sabha lives. Paul told me that when he first became aware of Sabha, he would sometimes watch as she walked along the road to and from the factory where she worked, and when he later saw her home he realized she lived in poverty.

But Sabha's story is truly amazing and deserves to be told. There are many blind and disabled people living in Bethlehem. But there are not many who are as grateful and joyous as Sabha Asmar. Look into her face and you quickly realize she has no eyes – her eyelids closed long ago. Yet her face radiates with life! She has a smile that lights up the darkest room.

She welcomed us as she heard us arriving. "Come in, come in!" she called. As we entered her room I saw a bed in one corner, a table and chair in another and through a curtain at the far end, a simple kitchen area; and somewhere there must have been a toilet. I asked Sabha about her life.

I was born in 1946 in a town called Tul Karem, which is north-west of Nablus. *(Nablus is the new name for the ancient biblical town of Shechem, situated north of Jerusalem. It lies at the heart of the West Bank of today which, in turn, is also known by its historic biblical name – the hills of Samaria.)*

My family is Muslim. As a four-year-old child, I lost my sight when I had measles. Looking back, I believe it was due to lack of proper care. My mother was divorced at the time and was not at home to look after me. When she realized I had gone blind, I was taken to a home for the blind run by Christians in a town called Beit Hanina, which is north of Jerusalem.

I don't really remember much about those days; I was only four and it is a long time ago now. But what I do remember is that I was there for eight years before anybody came to visit me. It was at this school that I learned about the Christian faith. Most of our teachers were also totally blind, just like me; others could see a little bit. One teacher in particular taught us the Bible and she told us the stories about Jesus. We learned about His childhood and how He grew up, and she explained how He was the one who came to earth to take away our sins by dying on the cross and then rising again, and how He is now interceding for us. I can honestly say that today I don't remember anything about Islam – I only know about the Christian faith.

I don't know whether you have heard about a lady called Helen Keller. She was born in Alabama in the United States of America, and when she was nineteen months old she contracted an illness which left her both blind and deaf. This was very difficult both for Helen and for her parents, and gradually, as she grew up, she turned into a very difficult child. Her parents found somebody to help her and gradually she learned to communicate using her hands, and then went on to learn the Braille language.

She became very interested in helping other blind and deaf people, and travelled to Israel in the 1950s and visited a school for the blind and deaf in Jerusalem. She was inquisitive and asked what the blind people she met there did once they had finished studying at school. She offered to help to build a home for adult blind people where they could be properly cared for and at the same time learn a trade so that they could earn a living. A home opened in Beit Hanina called the Helen Keller Home, and when I was eighteen years old, that was where I went to live.

In 1967, during the Six Day War, while I was at the Helen Keller Home, the English people who ran it (under the auspices of the Bible Lands˙ Society) gave us a choice: either we could return to our families for the duration of the war, or we could stay in Beit Hanina. This was difficult for me, because I didn't know my family any more – they never visited me or made contact in any way. My father had moved away and was making a new life for himself in Kuwait and had married another woman. By this time I was twenty-one and my faith was strong. I thought carefully about what I should do. I had a desire to be with my people. So I chose to go back to my family, who were now living in Jordan. My stepmother was there at the time, preparing to join my father in Kuwait.

But things did not work out as I had hoped. I lived with my stepmother for two years, and then my father returned from Kuwait to collect his wife, and he didn't approve of me going with them to Kuwait. I was moved to a town in Jordan called Irbid and once again I was on my own.

It was then that the Lord did a big miracle in my life. The Bible Lands Society sent some people to visit me in Jordan and when they saw my situation they realized it wasn't easy, so they offered to give me a permit to return to the West Bank.

But there was a big problem to overcome because I had lost my ID when I left Beit Hanina during the war, and in order to return to the West Bank I would need a visa.

Once again the Lord made a big miracle in my life by helping me to meet a German lady. She was a Christian. She said "Sabha, I will take you to the military governor." He was a Jewish man and I told him the story of how, in 1967, I had left Bethlehem to go and live with my family in Jordan to escape the war, believing that my father would look after me. I explained that my father had then moved to Kuwait and how I was left alone with nobody to help me. He listened patiently but told me that it was my family's responsibility to obtain a permit for me. But I told him that nobody in my family cared about what happened to me. It was then that the Lord worked on his heart, and through him I obtained my ID without having to go through a lot of difficulties. He just worked it out!

Today Sabha lives alone in Bethlehem. I asked her to describe an average week.

I have lived in this house for the past eleven years. When I first came here an American lady helped me to pay the rent, but when she was no longer able to help I found a job in a sewing factory where I earn a $100 a month. But of course, that is not enough to pay the rent. However, I have learned to trust the Lord and He has provided for all my needs.

My job at the factory involves finishing off the clothes after they have been sewn together. They bring me the finished garments inside out. I give each garment a good shake to get rid of any loose threads. Then I turn the clothes

135

the right way out and fold each garment carefully.

Every Sunday I go to a Presbyterian church – I have been going there for over twenty years. I like it there; the people are kind to me. They have offered to come and drive me there, but I have learned to walk to the church by myself; it only takes me fifteen minutes. But I am finding it increasingly difficult because so many cars are now parked on the pavements. Sometimes I feel embarrassed because people shout at me, "This way, that way!" But I don't like to be beholden to anyone, so I trust the Lord to help me, no matter how embarrassed I feel.

I asked Sabha whether she ever asked herself the question, "Why has all this happened to me?"

I do. But coming from a Muslim background, I believe the Lord has saved me for a purpose. After all, He has called me out from among my own people. The Bible promises that He will never leave me nor forsake me. I have been in so many different Christian homes and for the last eighteen years I have been living on my own and He has never left me nor forsaken me. He is always surrounding me. When I go to the factory – getting there by car, it seems so close – but of course, since I'm a blind person, it may take me up to ten minutes to walk from my house to the factory. But no matter how long it takes, He is always with me. I never feel that I am alone. He is always protecting me, and every morning I thank Him for His love and His mercies that are new every morning.

I have got two really close friends: Paul, who I have known for the past four or five years, and a lady from America who lived for over twenty years in Bethlehem before leaving the country. They are the two people who visit me. They sit with me and have a cup of tea.

I asked Sabha what she thinks when she looks to the future.

That is a difficult question. I don't think I have any future. Eight hours a day and six days a week I am with Muslim people at the factory. They are not open to the Word, so I feel I am struggling the whole time. So I live a day at a time and trust the Lord for that day. I don't have any profession to depend on.

The Lord is so close to me – I am not boasting. I tell my American friend how good the Lord is to me.

She replies, "But the Lord is good to everybody."

"No," I reply, "you can't imagine how close He is to me! I have no fear about living on my own or sleeping here alone. The Lord is with me."

When I was able to buy a television, I told the man who came to put up the satellite dish for me that I wanted only the Christian channels. I really enjoy listening to these channels. I don't need eyes because I have good ears to hear!

Every Sunday Paul visits me and brings me lunch. We watch the BBC together and if I have any questions, he helps me.

Sabha recently left her job at the factory and now works from home knitting shawls, which she sells.

Chapter 13
Dan and Dalia Alon

ighly qualified with lucrative jobs and a bright future – Dan and Dalia Alon wanted for nothing. Their three healthy, intelligent children were thriving intellectually and socially.

Dan was born into a secular Jewish family while Dalia was born into a traditional Jewish family who had lived in the land of Israel for several generations (from Dalia's mother's side). Dan's father was a career officer in the Israeli Defence Force (IDF). After completing his army service, Dan went to university where he studied industrial engineering, and for the next sixteen years he worked in this field.

However, despite enjoying the benefits of success, as the years passed Dan and Dalia realized they were searching for something deeper; they were searching for the meaning of life.

When they were offered the opportunity to leave Israel for a year to live in America, they didn't hesitate. Little did they realize it would be an experience that would change their lives for ever.

I travelled by train from Tel Aviv to Beersheva to meet Dan and Dalia. Today they live in the Negev desert in southern Israel in a town called Mitzpe-Ramon. They are retired now, but as is the case with many retired people, they are busy! In their case, they are working hard to encourage a small group of Israeli Russian-speaking believers who live in Mitzpe-Ramon. Although small in numbers, they have a huge vision; they believe their job is to pray for the body of believers in Israel today, and for other Israelis to come to faith in Yeshua, the Messiah.

Dan told the first part of their story.

Three years after we got married Dalia and I were looking for truth and how we could make our life better. So we started exploring and experimenting with various forms of spirituality. We tried yoga. We tried meditation. We went to seminars about the New Age movement in the hope that we would find what we were looking for. We felt as though something was missing in our lives that had nothing to do with material possessions; rather, our search was about finding something or someone to fill the spiritual void in our hearts and minds.

In the summer of 1991 I was given the opportunity by my employers to take a sabbatical for one year; so we decided, as a family, to go to America. We were looking forward to spending some of that time with a group of New Age followers on the west coast of America. Looking back, we can now see that God had a totally different plan for us.

We arrived in America in the early summer. Our children had been registered in schools there, beginning after the summer holidays. I was planning to undertake some research at a university beginning in the autumn, so before the summer vacation began, I did the necessary work in preparation for later in the year, leaving us free to enjoy some spare time together as a family.

A couple of weeks later, with preparations for the autumn in place, we were free to start exploring America! At first our trips were to nearby places. I remember we visited a nature reserve in the State of Oregon close to where we were staying. On the way we stopped to buy a new camera for Dalia. She immediately put it round her neck so that when we arrived at the nature reserve and parked the car, she would be ready. Little did we realize then that a camera would be the catalyst that would lead us to find a person who would provide the answers to the questions about truth and life that we were so desperately seeking.

There were some wonderful waterfalls in the state park. It was a vast place with a river running through it, and forests that we explored with our three children. We were very excited to have found such a spectacular place. As we were approaching one of the waterfalls, we saw a woman sitting on a nearby rock talking to somebody.

Dalia said to me, "Look, she has the same camera as me."

I said, "Dalia, what does it matter? We didn't come to look at cameras – we came to look at the waterfalls!"

But my wife didn't hear me and, being a very spontaneous person, she was already jumping over the rocks to speak to this woman! I was very embarrassed because our English was not very good at that time – we spoke "Israeli English"!

"Look, look," I heard Dalia say to her, "we have the same camera!"

I, meanwhile, turned towards our children to make sure they were safe – we had two young boys and a baby in a pram, and the boys were running around on a narrow trail. I called out to them in Hebrew, "Be careful!"

Then my wife called to me very excitedly, "Come over here, come, come!"

So I went over to join her and this lady, who looked at me with her big eyes and said in her broad American accent, "Wow, you're Jewish? You're from Israel? I'm Jewish too!" And she started to speak a few words in Hebrew, although she didn't speak the language fluently.

And so it was that she joined us as we walked through the park, and as we talked we were sure we had found a new candidate to join our New Age group! We told her all about our interest in the New Age and although she listened, she didn't express any real interest. Rather, she said only one thing: "I have a wonderful Father in heaven. He loves me so much."

As we talked we felt something radiating from her, although at that time we didn't understand what it was. She was short and overweight, and to be honest, she wasn't good looking! But something was attracting us to her and we felt we wanted to stay in touch with this lady. As we approached the car park and were getting ready to leave, we told her that in three months' time our son would be having his Bar Mitzvah and we would like to invite her to come. "OK, I'll come," she said. With that we exchanged addresses and telephone numbers and said goodbye and left.

Although we had spoken to her about our interest in the New Age movement, she hadn't said anything to us about her faith, other than mentioning that she had a wonderful Father in heaven! We had no idea who this was. Exactly what she believed remained a mystery to us.

A month and a half later Americans were celebrating one of their national holidays, which meant we had an extended weekend break. So we looked at the map to see where we could travel and decided to go to northern California. We planned to go to the Sequoia National Park to see the famous huge Sequoia trees there. As we planned our journey, we realized that this lady lived on the border of Oregon and northern California and our route would take us through the town where she lived! So we phoned her.

"Please come," came the reply. "You can stay with me overnight and then travel on the next day."

We arrived at her home on the Friday evening to find that she had invited a few of her friends to meet us and hear about Israel. We enjoyed a meal together and then went to bed. The next morning we got up and continued on our journey. Before we left, she insisted that we stay overnight with her on our way home.

"You can't travel a thousand miles in one day," she said. "You must come and stay with me again."

We thanked her and went on our way.

Two days later we arrived back at her house and stayed another night. She made us very welcome and was keen to hear what we had to say, but she still didn't say anything about her faith.

A month and a half later it was time for our oldest son's Bar Mitzvah. Our friend from Oregon arrived on the Friday evening. "I'm not going to stay with you," she told us. "You are very busy organizing the Bar Mitzvah and you have to be in the synagogue early in the morning. I have a good friend who lives nearby and it's an ideal opportunity for me to visit her."

So that Friday evening, we were sitting and talking and eating late into the night. Eventually we said we had to be in the synagogue early in the morning, so we had better get some sleep. It was then, just before she left, that she told us she believed in Yeshua. She shared some verses with us from Isaiah and Jeremiah. I believed there and then. "Today half the world believes in Him," I said, "so surely this is something that we should take seriously and consider for ourselves."

Dalia's immediate response to me was, "If you believe, I will believe too."

And so, without understanding anything, we were together in our new-found belief in Yeshua!

Now, we had grown up in Israel. When we first met this lady from Oregon we were in our forties and had never met a Jewish believer in Yeshua before. We had never read the New Testament. In fact, we had grown up with many negative attitudes about Christianity and about Jesus. And yet, something deep inside us told us that this lady was right and this was the truth.

As we tried to get to sleep that night, our minds were busy thinking about what we had heard. Then some doubts started to enter my mind: "Don't trust her. Don't believe her. She's trying to steal your money!" But I didn't listen to those doubts; instead I put them out of my mind.

The next day we were busy with the Bar Mitzvah and our friend went back to her home. Two weeks later she called us and we arranged to meet again. It was then that she gave us Bibles in Hebrew – the Old and the New Testaments separately.

As soon as we got back home we started to read our Bibles. It is important to understand that as Israelis we grew up studying the Old Testament only (the Tenach), albeit in a very secular, even atheistic, way. Many of the teachers in Israel who are teaching the Tenach are atheists – they do not believe what the Bible says. So I knew the Tenach. In fact, I loved studying it. But once I'd finished my time at school, the book was put on the shelf and started to gather dust. We had finished studying it, so it had no further use!

But now we started to read it again. Whilst I came from a secular Jewish family, I was open and very curious to read the New Testament. But Dalia, who came from a traditional Jewish family, hesitated to read it because while we were growing up it was a book that we had been forbidden (by the rabbis) to read – she could only imagine what her sister would say to her if she knew.

That first night back at home, I started to read the Gospel of Matthew while Dalia was reading the Old Testament. It wasn't long before I was amazed at what I was reading!

At the end of their twelve-month sabbatical in America, Dan and Dalia returned to Israel very different people. They settled back into Israeli life, living in the north of the country, and for a while they didn't know any other Jewish believers in Jesus. Eventually they made contact with a congregation in Tiberias, which they joined, and they remained there for several years. When the time came for them to retire, they felt it right to move to the south of Israel, to the Negev desert, and today they live in Mitzpe-Ramon where they are slowly building a Messianic congregation. Dan explained what is going on there today.

We are leading a very small group of mainly Russian-speaking Jewish believers, who are mostly women. But we don't worry about numbers. We know that the Lord has put us there and He wants us to be there. A little while ago I was sitting in our living room and asked the Lord, "What are we doing here? Why are we here? Why have you brought us here? Because it doesn't look as though much is happening."

And then I thought about Abraham and some questions came into my mind. What age was he when he came to Canaan? Seventy-five years old. And at what age did he pass away? One hundred and seventy-five. So how many years was he living in the land of Israel? One hundred years. What was he doing in the land during that time? As I thought about this I realized that, in some respects, he was "doing" nothing. He had made a big mistake with Ishmael. Then Isaac was born. He owned a lot of cattle and had become a very wealthy man. He was also a prayerful man, and everywhere he went he built an altar to the Lord.

It was then I heard the Lord say to me very clearly, "I didn't call you to *do*, I called you to *be*. You are here to *be* here and to pray and put your stamp here. What is going to be the result is my issue, my task."

After that experience I was able to relax. I could accept that if the Lord wanted our group to grow bigger, He would bring the people along. We would continue praying and trust the Lord to "do" the work.

I asked Dan, "When you think about the future and the bigger picture of what God is doing, what is your understanding of the days in which we are living?"

Let me put it this way: all the prophecies that are written in the Bible are concerned with Israel. The Lord has revealed to us through His Word what He is going to do here. We don't know the details, just the outline. I believe we have to keep serving Him faithfully here so that we are ready for when He returns. The Lord has given Dalia and me a deep desire to pray for the body of believers here in the land of Israel. We live in a very high place. Mitzpe-Ramon is the same height above sea level as Jerusalem – over 3,000 feet. The high places used to be places of prayer. We have opened our home as a place of prayer, so when people come to the desert to spend time with the Lord, they can stay with us.

Each week we meet with our group and we pray and study the Bible together. At the present time we are studying John's Gospel. We are still in the first chapter because there is a big argument amongst Jewish believers in Israel today about the divinity of our Lord, and the Gospel of John shows very clearly that Yeshua is God; He was and He is and He will be. We are living in times of great deception and the enemy will do all he can to upset and destroy the body of believers, and we need to be very careful. We have to discern between truth and lies, so it is very important that we learn to be still before the Lord and let Him teach us through His Word.

As for how Israel and the church fit together – to me, Israel without the church is like a chair with only two legs. We need to work together in partnership. The church around the world needs to know that Israel is important and we need the church to pray for us here. I know that there are believers who are suffering greatly in many places around the world, and it is very important to pray for them. At the same time, the Bible teaches us that Israel is the apple of God's eye, which means the devil is always trying to destroy us. There is much spiritual warfare here and we really need the prayers of the church in the nations.

Dalia then took up the story.

Living in the desert means we are far away from the majority of the population. It is quiet here and the pace of life is slow, so it is easier to concentrate on Him. We often go out into the desert to spend time with the Lord and we ask Him to speak to us and teach us. Since we came to the Negev we understand more clearly the calling on our lives. The history of Israel started in the Negev, where we live. Abraham was in Beersheva. Moses spent forty years travelling through the desert. In our case, we believe we are here to hear Him, to follow Him, to do His work and to build a group of believers who have on their heart to pray for the body of Christ in this land. As we all realize, the believers are under constant attack from the enemy and so we pray for protection for the body of Christ in Israel.

(It is worth noting that out of a population of 8 million people, approximately 12,000 Jewish people believe that Yeshua is the Messiah. This is a small percentage of the population, although the numbers are growing.)

Many Christians around the world pray for Israel. But I would urge them to pray specifically for the believers in Jesus who live here. Many congregations here are suffering from the attacks of the enemy, and I believe we need to be like Nehemiah, who built the walls around the city of Jerusalem to protect the people from the attacks of the enemy forces who were intent on their destruction.

We know that in the days to come the earth is going to be shaken; there will be more wars and earthquakes; the global economic situation will worsen and many people will become afraid. As we anticipate these events happening around us, we pray for the people we live amongst, that they will seek the Lord, and when they find Him we are here to help them. We are anticipating that many more Jewish people will come to believe in Yeshua in the coming days.

Chapter 14
Azar Ajaj and NETS

here are a number of churches in Nazareth dedicated to the Annunciation. The church that dominates Nazareth today is the vast modern Catholic Basilica of the Annunciation that was built over the cave that is believed to have been Mary's home. When you visit the church you can see this cave. Built over the earlier remains of Byzantine and Crusader churches, this church, the largest in the Middle East, was designed by the architect Giovanni Muzio and was consecrated in 1969. The much smaller and much older Greek Orthodox Church of the Annunciation is built right over the spring where it is believed that Mary met the angel Gabriel who announced to her that she was to be the mother of a son:

> *Do not be afraid, Mary, you have found favour with God. You will be with child and give birth to a son, and you are to give him the name Jesus. He will be great and will be called the Son of the Most High. The Lord God will give him the throne of his father David, and he will reign over the house of Jacob forever; his kingdom will never end.*
>
> *Luke 1:30–33*

The Nazareth Jesus knew would have been a very small village. Today, 2,000 years later, Nazareth is a large, bustling Arab town where Christian pilgrims come in their droves to visit these two churches in particular. But it's easy to miss what else goes on there, off the tourist trail.

Azar Ajaj is an Israeli Arab Christian. He was born and raised in Nazareth. As a young man he left the town to study at the Hebrew University in Jerusalem, before returning to work with a student organization run jointly by Jewish and Arab believers. He married a girl from Bethlehem and when I first met him a few years ago, he was the pastor of the Baptist church in Nazareth. He has faced many challenges being an Evangelical Christian leader in a predominantly Muslim town where the majority of Christians belong to the Orthodox and Catholic churches; he therefore knows what it is to be one of a minority within a minority. But Azar had an early taste of what it means to be in the minority when he became the first Christian in his family, at the age of fourteen.

My parents didn't like it very much but they accepted it. My brother became a believer at the same time as I did. A few years after that he started a Bible study at home and my parents became believers too.

I asked Azar why he decided to study at the Hebrew University in Jerusalem.

As Israeli Arabs, we grew up in Israel and we studied Hebrew at school; it is our second language. The Hebrew University is one of the many universities we were able to attend. I studied mathematics but I never worked as a mathematician because, after I finished my degree, God called me to work in a student ministry called the Fellowship of Christian Students in Israel. It was great, because Arab Christians and Jewish believers worked together to share their faith with other students on the campuses. I had a great time working with this ministry.

I found it interesting that as an Arab, Azar was prepared to work with Jews. This was his response:

Nazareth is situated in Galilee, in the northern part of the country. It is an Arab town with a population of 70,000. Two-thirds are Muslim and one-third call themselves Christian. However, these people are not necessarily believers; rather, they are nominal Christians, meaning they are neither Jewish nor Muslim! Although Nazareth was the hometown of Jesus, sadly, today there is not a large Evangelical Christian witness here. People know about Jesus but they do not know Him personally. The relationship between the Muslims and the Christians is calm at the moment, but there are underlying tensions which often come to the surface. There is pressure being a Christian here.

One of the challenges for both Jewish and Arab believers living in Israel, is to work together to show unity at a time when our country is facing very difficult challenges. Actually, I do not remember a time of peace, and today many people are losing hope. They don't trust the government and they don't trust the army; they don't trust anyone. Every time I open the Bible I see that God is calling us as believers to live in unity, and this unity should reflect His peace and the hope that the world can have through Him. I don't see any way to proclaim this peace to the people around us unless we as the body of Christ (and when I say "the body of Christ", I mean both Arab and Jewish believers in Israel) learn to live in unity and love, and work together to reflect His peace and hope to the people in the country.

It is very challenging. God is moving and there are great things happening. Recently we had a meeting in which many Arab congregations and many Messianic Jewish congregations came together for a picnic in a forest. Around 8,000 people attended. An Arab pastor preached and a Messianic Jewish pastor preached and we expressed our love and unity together. So it is very important for people around the world to understand that it is through the unity of Messianic and Arab believers that the peace of God will be proclaimed in Israel.

More recently, in 2011, I visited Azar again in Nazareth. He is no longer the pastor of the Baptist church. Now he is the Dean of Students and one of the lecturers at the Nazareth Evangelical Theological Seminary (or NETS for short). As Dean he is responsible for the spiritual welfare of students, and as a lecturer he teaches mainly pastoral care and Old Testament studies. NETS is the realization of a dream Azar had some years ago, so I asked him to explain his vision.

NETS started five years ago and our vision for the school has three elements. First, we want to bring a high theological standard of teaching to our students. We need our future leaders to know the Bible and have sound theological understanding. I believe that without such training, the Evangelical churches have no future! Secondly, we are not just interested in our students achieving high academic standards; we are also very interested in their spiritual development and leadership skills. Regarding leadership, we strive to train our students to become "servant" leaders here in the country, able to set a good example and having the heart of Jesus to serve the people here. The third pillar of our vision is to encourage reconciliation among the body of Christ; here that means reconciliation between Evangelical Arab Christians and Messianic Jewish believers in Yeshua.

Although we do not have any Messianic Jewish students studying with us (yet), it is still an important part of our vision and we hope to be able to welcome Jewish students in the future. However, we do have two Messianic Jewish teachers who are working with us. We are always looking for ways to encourage unity within the body of Christ here in Israel. One of the reasons we do not have Jewish students is because Nazareth is an Arab town and Jewish people do not live here. It is a remarkable achievement that we have two Messianic Jewish lecturers who are prepared to travel long distances to Nazareth to come and teach here. This reflects their desire to be a part of this vision.

I then spoke to some of the students, beginning with Ziad. He has been studying at NETS for four years. What makes Ziad's story so interesting is that he is blind and so has to have somebody to be his "eyes". May is helping him. She is from Glasgow in Scotland and is the wife of Revd Dr J. Bryson Arthur, the Principal of NETS. She described how she helps Ziad.

Throughout the course, Ziad has several essays to complete. Together we find the reference books he needs to study. I read the books to him and he listens; he has an exceptionally good memory. Once he has decided what he wants to write, we start. As he dictates, I write; and when we have finished I read it back to him, and if there are any gaps he fills them in and I write some more!

It is clear that this is a lesson in perseverance. So I asked Ziad to tell me why he is doing all this study.

I have a calling from God for ministry. I am one of the leaders in my church and do a lot of pastoral work and preaching, as well as leading worship. I believe God brought me to NETS to equip me with everything I need to fulfil His calling in my life.

Ziad is married and he and his wife have a young family. In fact when I met him, his wife had just given birth to their second child. So was Ziad born and brought up in Nazareth?

I was born in Tur'an, a village near Nazareth. It is situated between Cana of Galilee and Tiberias. I am thirty-three years old and have been a Christian for fifteen years. It is important for me that we, as Evangelical Arab Christians, have good relationships with our Messianic Jewish brothers, and so I am glad that here at NETS there is a strong emphasis on reconciliation and how real peace and unity can only be achieved through Jesus Christ. When I am in a lecture that is being given by a Jewish believer, I find it really interesting because it brings a fresh perspective to our thinking and understanding.

I then met Atom, who came to Israel from Southern Sudan to escape the war there. Whilst he is living in Israel as a refugee, it is clear from his story that he believes he has a destiny to fulfil. Azar explained that Atom was introduced to him by the leader of a Messianic congregation in Jerusalem who, realizing God had His hand on Atom's life, asked Azar to train him for the ministry – they were not able to help him at the congregation in Jerusalem because Atom did not speak Hebrew at that time, only Arabic. Since then he has learned to speak Hebrew and English. Atom is wasting no time; he has already started a church in Tel Aviv by himself, which he pastors. Azar told me that he had been there a few times to preach and that he was amazed to see what God is doing amongst the people in the congregation. Azar told me:

We are very happy to have Atom with us at NETS, and we look forward to seeing what God has planned for his future. Atom graduated in December 2011, and he is preparing to go back to Southern Sudan to fulfil God's call on his life and start a church there. It has been a great privilege to work with and train this man of God.

I put it to Azar that it's clear they have a cross-section of students at NETS, so what are their aims as they look to the future?

Yes, our goal is to prepare our students for what God is going to do in the future here in Israel. We are pleasantly surprised that God has brought us students like Atom, all the way from Southern Sudan! But I do not care about how many students we have at NETS. Rather, in five or ten years' time, when we look back at how our students have developed, we want to see that they are working in the ministry, reaching out to local people, regardless of whether those people are Muslim, Jewish or Christian. We want to see them taking their place as an integral part of the Evangelical ministry in the country.

I turned again to Ziad. He already has a number of degrees, including a Master's in Special Education. I asked him what he believes God is doing in Israel at this time.

After a gap of 2,000 years, I believe God is building His Kingdom here once again. We in the Arab community believe that God is preparing us for a new awakening amongst the Muslim population here. We need to have His love in our hearts. We need to know the Bible. We need to be good servants. After all the degrees that I have, I believe the key issue in Christianity and ministry has nothing to do with degrees; rather, it is about the heart. I believe the key is having the right heart combined with diligent study of the Word of God; the Word of God with the anointing of the Spirit, together. God is looking for people here in the Holy Land who can serve Him in humility and love and with hard work.

I then met Bishara Deeb, another student at NETS. A married man with three grown daughters, he was born in Nazareth and went to the Baptist School, where he met his wife. Bishara told me:

She was in my class. We fell in love and got married five years later.

When I was a young man I wanted to leave Israel. I

dreamt about going to live in Spain or Greece to have a new start in life. I was tired of the political situation here. You need a lot of energy to keep going, day by day, living with all the pressure in this land. Most of us have dreamt at some time that we would like to leave the Middle East and find a more peaceful life somewhere else.

But I am still here! I believe the hand of God was on my life from the beginning. Twenty years ago I was ready to move to Spain – I had made all the arrangements and was just waiting for my passport when at the last minute, I was prevented from going. I wondered then whether God wanted me to be here; now I am sure!

At first I was very disappointed when those plans did not work out. But after I became a Christian and looked back on those days, I thanked God. Now I know it was a good thing that happened, even though it caused me some pain. I know it was from Him for His glory. Today it is amazing how strongly I feel about not leaving Israel!

I owned a grocery shop in those days in the main street in Nazareth. It was a good business. After I became a Christian I started to minister to people through my work at the shop. I distributed leaflets that talked about Jesus. I started visiting people in their homes, and gradually I decided this was something I wanted to do more. By this time I was working alongside other Christians who were training me in how to talk to people about Jesus.

When I heard clearly from God that this was the main thing He wanted me to do, I started thinking about how I could leave my work in the shop. It wasn't easy for my wife and me. Israel is an expensive country and we were concerned about how we could cover our living costs. We started praying more earnestly and one day God told us very clearly that now was the time to leave the business.

So after four years, I closed the business and started a new life as a full-time Christian worker. At first I was afraid and couldn't fully trust God! But He waited one year for me and my wife to trust Him; He was very kind to us. Even though we struggled financially, still we were sure we were being obedient to what God wanted us to do.

After I left the shop I started to visit people in their homes and I faced many hard questions that I had difficulty in answering. I felt I needed to learn more about the Bible, and when Dr Bryson (the Principal of NETS) invited me to join the college, I agreed that it would be a good thing for me to do. I have been studying here for four years now and my knowledge of the Bible has increased so much. It has opened my mind in so many ways, especially in the areas of preaching and evangelism.

I asked Bishara to look forward into the future – what did he anticipate he would be doing and where?

My dream is to have The Harvest – that is the name of my ministry now – established in Israel in such a way that I can develop teams of workers that combine local people with volunteers from abroad. I would like them to come and live here and get to know the community, learn the language and culture, and start working with me in the many Muslim villages around here, because I believe these people need to see and hear the gospel. I have the vision to do this in a new way – to live there, amongst the people. By living with them, we can show them the love of God as well as teaching them about the Bible. So I hope and pray that we will soon have churches for these Muslim people.

Sometimes you need to do more than tell people the story. They have many physical needs and we see that we can both answer the physical needs of the people and answer their spiritual needs. It's not easy to go into the Muslim villages. I discovered that first we need a prayer strategy and then we can start talking with people. I visit the villages with people who will be working alongside me, working and preaching the gospel there. We pray – at first we do nothing except pray. Sometimes we spend two days praying in the same place. People there start to recognize us and they start to ask us what we are doing. So we tell them we want to share with them about the love of God and the message of the gospel. They are always very interested and they want to know more, because not many people visit these Muslim places. They invite us into their homes and serve us coffee and sometimes cakes, and they are always very interested in what we have to say and about whom we talk.

Clearly, Bishara has been encouraged by the open hearts and minds that the people living in the Muslim villages in northern Israel have towards the gospel. So I asked him what he is expecting God to do in the future.

I look at the Evangelical churches here and I believe we work hard, but I also believe that sometimes we need to have a new vision. I think God wants us to be more courageous and take the gospel to people we think will refuse it. Sometimes we all work in the same place and we go around and around doing small things, but there are Jewish and Muslim places that we

161

need to visit to open doors there. That is what I believe God wants us to do here. We need to just open our eyes and look two kilometres down the road to the people living there.

My message to Christians in the West reading this book is firstly to ask them to pray for us. Then, when they start to take a prayerful interest, I would encourage them to come and visit us in order to find out more about the Evangelical Arab Christians who try hard to live in Israel and to preach the gospel here. Then, when they have met us, I hope they will begin thinking about coming to help us with evangelism! We already have teams coming to perform musical shows in the streets. We have other teams coming to teach English and sport. I would like to see this increase. We are trying to use every talent and every gift that God has given us to tell the people in Israel about Jesus and His love.

For more information about the Nazareth Evangelical Theological Seminary, visit www.nazarethseminary.org

Chapter 15
Ofer Amitai

The challenge of bringing news and information about events in the Middle East to a Christian audience is to find a way of reporting what is happening in an unbiased and accurate manner, whilst at the same time putting those events and happenings into a biblical context.

Many of the stories in this book are pure testimony – God's dealings with individuals to change their heart and give them the heart and mind of Christ. Other stories combine testimony with biblical teaching and prophetic insight. This chapter falls into that category.

I first met Ofer Amitai in 1999. After living in the United States for a period of time, he had returned to Israel several years before, bringing his American wife and young family with him. As his story reveals, he left Israel after serving his time in the army, which for Ofer included a serious injury and war. He needed to "clear his head" and find the meaning of life. Nothing could have prepared him for what was to happen next.

Today Ofer is the leader of a congregation in Jerusalem and has also established the Israel Prayer Centre. He is intent on praying for the Kingdom of God to come: on earth, in Israel, and the surrounding nations.

Ofer was born in 1951 in Tel Aviv. His father, who had immigrated to Israel from Poland in 1935, became a distinguished officer in the Israeli Defence Force. His mother's family had been in Israel for several generations. Ofer grew up in a secular Zionist family. Like the majority of Israelis, he served in the army. It was during this time, in 1973, that the Yom Kippur War broke out, and Ofer experienced the trauma of front-line action. When his time in the army was completed, he left Israel and travelled – eventually as far as India.

I met Ofer to record this interview at the Israel Prayer Centre, which is situated in the Talpiot neighbourhood of Jerusalem. I asked him if we could record not only his personal story, but also his perspective on the bigger picture of why Israel is so important to God, and what is going on from a spiritual point of view. I knew of his concern that Christians living outside Israel often have a biased view of the conflict in the Middle East. He had earlier told me that unless Christians have an accurate biblical understanding of what God is doing in these days, their prayers may be ineffectual because they may not line up with God's will and purpose; they risk praying for what they want to happen!

By the time you read this chapter (unless you are one of those people who read the end of a book before the beginning), you will have read many inspiring stories of Jewish believers and Arab or Palestinian Christians living in Israel and the West Bank today, who not only have a powerful testimony of their own to share, but who also understand their Bibles and carry God's heart for the region.

The purpose of this chapter is to develop the prophetic angle even further, to bring revelation and understanding to help Christians in the nations relate to and become involved with God's passion for Israel and the Jewish people, to see them not only restored to the Land but also restored to God. The outcome of that will, as Ofer explains towards the end of this interview, impact the world in a way hitherto unseen.

As with all good stories, we start at the beginning, and ask the question, who and what have shaped the life of Ofer Amitai?

I was born and raised here in Israel, but grew up with deep questions as to the meaning of life. I wanted to know the truth. The questions that I harboured brought me to an impasse when I was injured during my military service. I faced death, and some of my friends did die. Later, I participated in the 1973 Yom Kippur War. I believe that anyone who has ever fought in a war comes out of the experience with deep questions. In my case, the search for answers to those questions led me on a journey that took me to America, where I went to university, and eventually to India, to study in an ashram. It was there, after despairing of yoga, a form of Hinduism, that I began to cry out to a God who I was not sure even existed.

After I had been seeking God in the midst of that very dark and oppressive "spiritual" environment, the Lord actually appeared to me. He came to me and spoke to me very clearly. He revealed Himself as the sovereign Creator. It is difficult to describe His authority. It is absolute. It is complete. It is supreme over all things. Yeshua's total victory on the cross means He has authority over all principalities and powers. This was communicated to me, and to this day I remain overwhelmed by it. But when the Lord spoke to me, together with this revelation of absolute authority, He spoke as a lowly servant. Those who have been to India will understand how low a servant is. Today, over thirty-five years later, these revelations continue to penetrate my life, and I understand more and more who God is.

On the heels of that experience I returned home for six months. The Messianic movement existed in Israel at that time, but it was very small and I was not aware of it. I felt the Lord leading me to go to the United States, primarily to find people who could help me grow in God. After a few months, the Lord called me to serve Him, though I didn't understand exactly what that would mean. I met Chris, who was to become my wife, and together we went to a small Bible school in Zion, Illinois in 1980, where we remained for fourteen years.

When we came to Jerusalem in 1994 I felt I was "equipped" for ministry. I was back in the midst of my people! But what did God want me to do? Not surprisingly, I felt Him say that I should simply wait on Him, sit at His feet, and that as I did, He would show me His perspective of what I was seeing. I was not to rush around in my own ability, or according to my own understanding. We had two school-aged children, and my family needed to learn Hebrew and find their way in Israeli society. They needed time and my support rather than being thrown into a flurry of activity and service. Looking back on those days, it was a very precious time with the Lord, and I continue in the same vein to this day, because I don't believe we ever grow out of the need of waiting on God and seeking His face.

We hadn't been here long before Chris and I inherited a small youth group, which began to grow and became inter-congregational. It was a wonderful season and a very sweet work. We would take the young people hiking and into the desert. We would worship together and talk about the Lord. It was a simple thing. The parents of some of the youth got acquainted with us and invited us to become pastors of their small congregation. After prayer and consideration we began to lead that group in 1997.

Since then we've gone through metamorphosis. At first the congregation grew very quickly, quadrupling in size in one year. But it was not a cohesive group; Jerusalem is made up of a multitude of people who each have their own ideas of what a congregation should be! Some were very concerned with traditional Jewish expression, whilst others insisted on something ultra-charismatic, and that describes just two of the camps.

We have worked through various processes and today the congregation is a very cohesive group of people who basically desire two things: first, to seek God and love Him with all their heart, and second, to lay down their lives in loving each other. That is what a congregation should be, and out of that stems everything else. We emphasize that I, as the leader, am not the congregation. Neither is the congregation an organization; rather, together we make up a congregation, a body, and each one has their part and contribution. Non-participation is not an option!

We believe the congregation is a place of transformation; the Lord, in His special way, is challenging people to be completely His, to give in fully to Him. If we are not careful, we can be Christians in name and not in content. Even 95 per cent of me is not enough – not for Him. We are a maturing congregation. We have some serious people who love the Lord. Everyone participates. We are very honest with each other – our culture is to be open – and in the Light we enjoy wonderful fellowship.

I asked Ofer about the Israel Prayer Centre.

The goal of the Israel Prayer Centre is to *pray*: to stand before the Lord in intercession for His Kingdom purposes, both for Israel, and for the larger picture of which Israel is a key. This includes the nations of the world. We also utilize this centre as a training place; we are keen on investing in young adults and training them to know the Lord and His purposes, as they relate specifically to the days in which we are living. In order to be effective before God, we have to pray with faith and understand what He is doing.

Ofer is also involved with Arab pastors; reconciliation is very much on his agenda. He explains:

We are involved with Arab brothers both in the Land and abroad. We cannot share about this in detail because of security concerns. Nevertheless, I have always believed that true reconciliation is based on God Himself: on His Word, His light and His truth, rather than initially on personal relationships. For years I had longed for genuine reconciliation in the hope that we would be able to stand together before the Lord, both Jews and Arabs, for God's plan. This is an awesome and powerful thing. Over the years we have been involved with Arab brothers who, through their own journeys with the Lord, and without any influence from us, have come to believe that God is restoring Israel. We have reached the point together in which, regardless of the political problems and without giving Him a detailed agenda on how He should accomplish it, we can stand before the Lord for the fullness of His purposes! This is a key issue because we are not just a group of believers; rather, we represent two peoples. We have learned how important it is to come together in a spirit of worship. We pray together for one another and care about each other's families. We care about each other's congregations and support them in whatever way we can. Our fellowship, respect and love for one another are very sweet because we share a precious faith.

In 1994, when Ofer and his family arrived in Israel, there were relatively few Messianic believers. Here he describes the growth he has seen.

Today there are approximately 88 Arab congregations and 200 Messianic Jewish congregations in Israel. Some of these are smaller house groups. Looking back, we can see that this growth began in the late sixties and early seventies with an outpouring of the Holy Spirit. This is very encouraging.

So what is God doing here? I believe that the Lord is doing just what He said He would do! He promised to bring us back to the Land and, most importantly, restore us to Himself. The existence of the Israeli body of believers is a clear demonstration of the Lord fulfilling His Word. We are a token; we are the first fruits and it is very encouraging. I have always believed that it is God's intention to make Israel a blessing in the midst of the earth, and our neighbours will benefit from that. God is not just working with the Jewish people; He is working in the entire region.

That prompted me to ask: Is it just a coincidence that there are Arabs living here? Some might question whether God knew what He was doing.

Now we are getting into muddy water! This area is so filled with emotion. It is hard to speak about it in a way that would be palatable to everyone. I can only speak from my own point of view. I have tried to refrain from fixing things for God or from being His counsellor. The Lord is the Lord. The reality of what I see is complex. I cannot solve the problems and challenges with my own intellect, but I can express things that I believe are true. For example, I believe that it is God who is bringing the Jewish people back to their homeland. Of course, I also recognize that there are Arab people living within these borders. Some are Israeli Arabs – those who remained in 1948, when the modern State of Israel was born, and have continued to live among us. Then there are the Palestinians living in the West Bank, those who left their properties, contrary to the plea of the nascent government, and responded to the call of the Arab world to flee. Nevertheless, regardless of this complex reality, I believe God is continuing with His plan and in the end it will be a blessing. When we look at the Bible we see that God's Word has often been fulfilled through times of crisis and conflict. I would add here that the ultimate conflict is not between Arabs and Israelis; rather it is between God and the world and the spirit of this world. There is something beyond the Arab/Israeli problem. The Bible is clear; the nations are not about to cooperate with God, nor will they welcome Him with applause; rather, they will resist Him.

God knows what He is doing and He has a solution. I

believe He is compassionate and loving. We read, "God so loved the world" (John 3:16) – that includes us all – and yet I cannot make God into an image that suits me, or ignore the Scriptures, or try to adjust them to fit my humanistic sentiments. It is very clear: God said He would bring the Jewish people back to the Land that He gave them as an eternal inheritance. In fact, He promised that He would bring us back, even in our sins. The wonderful thing is, He has promised to reveal Himself; He has promised to cleanse us; He has promised to pour out His Spirit upon us. All of this is in order to bring us back to Himself personally.

So what is the role of the church in the nations in all of this? What would you say to them?

These are very deep questions and the answers cannot be distilled into a soundbite. Before I can answer the question of what the church should do, I have to ask myself, "What has the church become?" – because I don't believe it is in the place where God wants it to be. I often say to Christians, "So you believe in Israel's restoration. Well, you are not going to be of any help to the plan of God if you are not walking with the Lord, and have infighting in your own church, or if you are in sin."

What is the condition of the church? I have lived abroad for long enough to be able to say that I believe, generally speaking, the church is in a catastrophic condition. You may ask, "What should the church do?" What she should be able to do is stand before the Lord and fulfil God's own call for her. But instead of that, the church has taken sides, or been affected by Replacement Theology,[1] or imbibed other viewpoints that make it impossible for her to clearly understand the issue from God's perspective. To me, the problem is manifold.

I am frequently asked to speak about Israel, but in all honesty, I most often end up speaking about the Lord Himself and people's need of Him. I share how He has transformed our congregation, how He has changed us as we have sought to live in the light and to please Him rather than ourselves, and the effect is electrifying.

The church in the nations needs to be revived and cleansed. She needs to be corrected and purified. Multitudes are seeking revival. But most often they are seeking power instead of purity or a closer relationship with God. The church cannot be a great help to God as long as she remains in her present condition.

However, I believe that there is another aspect to your question which relates to Christians as citizens of the nations, and as such, having political power and influence. The church's stand in the world of politics should be guided by biblical truth as it pertains to Israel and God's agenda. But if the church does not know God, or His heart, it becomes heavily influenced by politics and opinions. Rather than get her cue from heaven, the church has been deeply influenced by the world. And when the church becomes overly influenced by world politics, I wonder where she is with God. I am not questioning people's salvation – that is not my place – but do we see the world through the lens of politics or do we identify with a Kingdom perspective?

---

1. Replacement Theology states that because Israel failed and rejected Jesus as Messiah, God has rejected her and replaced her with the church. Israel therefore no longer has any place in God's plan for the redemption of mankind, and is today irrelevant.

The church, or at least a remnant, must come into a priestly relationship with God. I believe that the great mandate of the church in the nations is to stand before God for God's agenda. This is not easy, but if she is to be of any weight or consequence to God, she must come to this place. Without attempting to solve the regional problems between peoples, our primary obligation is to stand before the Lord over His Word until He performs it. It is not essential that we understand its outworking altogether.

I asked Ofer what he believes God's agenda is at this time.

I have to go back and ask, "What has God's purpose been from the beginning?" When I read from Genesis through to the book of Revelation, I see that God's desire has always been to redeem mankind from sin and death. God's unfolding plan is very clear and simple. To understand it, we must travel back many centuries to the time of Abraham. God chose a man, and supernaturally made him into a nation. God chose that nation as representative of mankind, and worked with them to bring the knowledge of sin by the law. By their inability to keep His law, God brought the understanding of the need of a Saviour; and ultimately, He brought forth His Saviour and His salvation through them.

Replacement Theology states, "You (Israel) have failed; you did not recognize the Messiah; you even betrayed Him." However, Paul's letter to the Romans makes it clear that this failure was God's plan, and that Israel would ultimately be restored, and recognize her Messiah. If I pose the question, "Did Yeshua have to die in order to provide atonement for sin; did the Lamb of God need to be crucified?" – every believer would answer in the affirmative. We understand that this was the will of God from the foundation of the world. And the Messiah could not have been crucified except in Israel, by the nation that acted on behalf of mankind as priest, within the framework of the system of sacrifices and blood atonement. The rejection and delivering up of the Messiah 2,000 years ago was part of God's economy, and Israel has had to bear the consequences for her role – or if you prefer, the punishment for it. It is a great mystery. But we have not yet seen the end of the story.

God promised to make a new covenant with the house of Israel and with the house of Judah after their failure to keep Sinai's covenant, according to Jeremiah 31. That new covenant was initiated with the blood of the Messiah, as Yeshua proclaimed when he lifted the cup before His Jewish disciples at the Passover meal on the eve of His betrayal. While the Jewish people as a nation rejected the Messiah, the first body of believers and its apostolic leadership were all Jews. Paul reveals in his letter to the Romans that there would always remain a remnant in Israel, even if unrecognized by the world and the church. God has always had a portion of believing Israel for Himself. God said that in the last days He would resurrect the nation, and He would restore Israel, as a nation, to Himself before fulfilling the rest of His agenda. This is clear both in the New Testament and in the prophets. The "times of the Gentiles" that Paul mentions in Romans began with the destruction of the second temple and the dispersion of the Jewish people in AD 70.

Because of God's love for the entire human race, He has provided time for the gospel to be preached to every nation on earth. God will continue to save people throughout the world, but the centre of His workings and His agenda is now positioned once again on this nation of Israel. In the last 150 years or so, the return of the Jewish people to the Land, the establishment of the modern State of Israel in her ancient homeland and inheritance, the reunification of Jerusalem, and the revival of the Messianic Jewish movement, are all signs that point to this.

The stumbling-block for many, as I mentioned before, is that Israel is not yet a holy people, serving the Lord. But God's promise is clear that He would gather His people and *then* pour upon them the Spirit of grace and supplication. The repentance and spiritual revival that this will bring in the midst of this nation will be what Romans calls "life from the dead" (Romans 11:15) for the Gentiles. The Scriptures do not exaggerate; the impact upon the world will be phenomenal.

I do not believe God's passion can ever be adequately described merely in general terms such as "He loves mankind." God loves each one of us as individuals, and that personal love for us is evident in the faithfulness in which He deals with us and cares for us. God's longing and plan to bring His people Israel back to Himself is clearly stated in the Scriptures. So whilst it is true that His passion is for *all* of mankind, He also faithfully remembers and continues to work with the nation that He chose to reveal Himself to and through, and that He used to bring forth the redemption of all peoples. I think when Christians look at the entirety of God's plan from the beginning, it becomes clear that God had to choose a nation; Yeshua had to be born into a specific family. If God has been careful to carry out His plan thus far, surely He will fulfil the rest of it unto completion.

I put it to Ofer that he has witnessed a great deal since returning to Israel in 1994. So I asked him to describe what he is anticipating will be happening in the next few years.

I can tell you what I'm praying for! One of the central things that I believe is burning in the heart of God is found in Zechariah 12:10:

> *I will pour out on the house of David and on the inhabitants of Jerusalem a spirit of grace and supplication. They will look on me, the one they have pierced, and they will mourn for him as one mourns for an only child, and grieve bitterly for him as one grieves for a firstborn son.*

Here the prophet speaks in the first person; it is as though God breaks through the human veil, the vehicle of the prophet. I believe that this displays His passion. It is similar to the story in Genesis where Joseph weeps in the back room as he waits to reveal himself to his own brothers. God is longing for this day, and I am longing also.

If I look to politics, I do not find a solution for the problems in our region. If I look at the prospect of continuing wars, it horrifies me to think how much bloodshed is yet to come. But ultimately, I have to hang on to God's goodness and sovereignty, and His ability to intervene in and interrupt human history. I am not talking about the Second Coming; it would be too complicated to try to understand end-time theology – there are many! But I believe God's heart is to reveal Himself to His people. The Scriptures clearly speak of Him gathering us to the Land and then revealing Himself to us. How? I don't know, and in some ways I don't care; I just long for it. I want to believe that God will intervene in human history and in our nation's history to reveal Himself. Can you imagine it? When this does happen, it will bring Israel finally to the point of realizing her destiny. That is what we are praying for, and we hang on to the fact that God aims to sanctify His name. That is the first desire of God that appears in the Lord's Prayer: "Hallowed be Your name. Let Your Kingdom come. Let Your will be done, on earth as it is in heaven."

Yeshua is always controversial. He will not yield to your political ideas, no matter on which side you put yourself. God is God, and I go back to the revelation I had of Him as absolute and supreme authority. He has the right and authority to do whatever He wants. Let Him draw the borders. That will be OK! Whatever portion He gives us, I will take. And whatever portion He gives the Palestinians, I believe they too will welcome.

God's passion and intent is to sanctify His name and remove the utter confusion, the Babylon of spiritual darkness covering the earth regarding who He is. We are all going to be humbled. The day of the Lord spoken about in Isaiah chapter 2 is the humbling of all things, and the exaltation of only *one*: God Himself, the Lord.

I asked Ofer what it means to him to pray for the peace of Jerusalem.

"Peace" in Hebrew means "completion", and that is what I pray for. To pray for the peace of Jerusalem is to pray for the fulfilment of God's agenda, for the fullness of His plan to unfold, both physically and spiritually. It is enough that we pray and ask Him to do what He said. I often pray, "Don't be limited by my understanding, Lord. Please, if I need more understanding, give it to me. But take my words as I pray Your Word, and accomplish it to the ultimate extent so that Your Kingdom comes and Your will is done."

Postscript

The Story of the Olive Tree Reconciliation Fund

T he people you have met through reading the stories in this book have, I hope, given you not only a desire to pray more, but also a desire to be involved in practical ways. As I mentioned in the opening pages, the most important question that *The Olive Tree* programme asks is, "What is God doing in Israel and the Palestinian Areas of the Holy Land today?"

As you have read, He is moving in the lives of individual believers in quite remarkable and unexpected ways. It is therefore true that "God works in mysterious ways His wonders to perform"!

So if, having read the stories in this book, you are feeling that you would like to help in some way, let me now tell you the story of the Olive Tree Reconciliation Fund (OTRF). I could never have imagined starting a charity, but that is what happened in 2008 as a direct result of people sending me gifts of money to pass on to the Jewish and Arab believers living in

Israel and the Palestinian Areas that they had been reading about in books or articles I had written.

In the beginning

It all started with an article about the plight of Arab Christians in Bethlehem – in particular, those belonging to the Evangelical community there. For those of you who are passionate about supporting Israel, this article posed a challenge: Can we feed first and talk theology afterwards? As I wrote then:

> *I am not saying that theology does not matter. Of course it does. Those who disagree with Replacement Theology (as I most certainly do) will never change the situation in Bethlehem by taking a stand-offish attitude. We have to go there, whether in prayer or in person, and get our hands dirty and help the people – otherwise there will soon be no Christian Arabs left in Bethlehem.*

The article went on to describe the heartache experienced by one Evangelical pastor in particular, and the sacrificial way in which he helped the people there, both Christians and Muslims.

The response to that article was overwhelming – and every penny donated was sent to the pastor in Bethlehem for him to give to those in need. It demonstrated that Christians in the UK who love Israel and the Jewish people, also love and support the Arab Christians and recognize the work of reconciliation that is going on between Arab Christians and Messianic Jewish believers in the Holy Land today.

Muslim Arabs have to taste Jesus, Jewish people have to see Him

I have written much about Labib Madanat, the team leader of Bible Society ministry in both Israel and the Palestinian Areas (his story is told at the beginning of this book). From a Jordanian family, he works with both Arab and Jewish believers as they take the gospel to both religious and secular Jews, as well as to Muslim Palestinians. In an earlier book (*A Future for Israel*), I wrote:

> *Labib knows from years of experience that true love and concern is primarily practical. "Muslim Arabs have to taste Jesus," he told me, "Jewish people have to see Him."*

In various articles I shared a couple of projects, ways in which Christians in the nations could support Labib Madanat and his teams, including those working in Gaza. And once again, people gave generously.

So when news broke about the murder of Rami Ayyad in October 2007, hearts were open, and the plight of his young widow, Pauline (who was expecting their third child), and their two young children prompted another flush of generosity. Rami was the manager of the Bible Society bookshop in Gaza City. He was kidnapped one Saturday afternoon in October 2007 as he was closing the shop.

Concerned he was late home, Pauline described how she had called her husband on his mobile phone. Rami replied to say he had been "delayed" and might be late. Pauline realized something was wrong and called Rami's brother, who also called Rami on his cell phone. Rami replied and managed to tell his brother that he was being held by a group and would be "away for a long time". After that the phone was switched off. Rami's body was found the next morning. He had been tortured before being murdered, after which his body was dumped.

The response to Rami's death, especially from Messianic Jewish believers living in Israel, has been unprecedented. A special fund has been established to support Pauline and her three children (she gave birth to a baby daughter shortly after Rami's death). The pain remains. Rami did not die in vain. But the needs are ongoing.

Persecution

In March 2008 Ami Ortiz, the teenage son of Messianic pastors David and Leah Ortiz, was cruelly injured when he opened what looked like a gift of food kindly left on the doorstep of the family's apartment in Ariel, Samaria. But it wasn't a gift; it was a bomb that blew up in Ami's face and almost killed him. Ami's recovery has been slow and painful. His medical bills have been huge. Once again readers responded generously, and today Ami has made a miraculous recovery.

Helping the stranger

During 2008 I wrote about the plight of Sudanese refugees in Israel and how one Messianic Jewish believer, Rita Tsukahira, found herself providing a refuge for these beleaguered people. Today, the question of helping the large numbers of African refugees pouring into Israel has become a national issue. As Rita said:

They have escaped from the devastation of the twenty-year war perpetrated on the Southern Sudanese people by the radical Islamic government in Khartoum, and the current genocide taking place in Darfur. Most had sought refuge in Egypt but found persecution and danger there as well. So, risking everything and paying hundreds of dollars to Bedouin guides, they were taken to the border with Israel and left to cross over into the desert in the dark of night. After walking for hours, Israeli soldiers would find the refugees and bring them to the base. As Sudan is an "enemy nation", they were considered a security risk and taken to prison. The army and the immigration police had no facility to care for the women and children. When I received the call, it was as if the Lord spoke a clear word to me: "This is going to be big." I had no idea that for more than a year, we would be the only place to take in Sudanese women and children. Both Muslim and Christian women from a number of different tribes in Sudan were sent to us. Many were traumatized by the events they had witnessed previously – the destruction of their villages, the killing of family members, rape and imprisonment. Through persistent prayer and consistent application of God's principles, we began seeing genuine spiritual transformation in the lives of women from both Christian and Muslim backgrounds.

One new man

More recently I have written about The House of Victory (Beit Nitzachon in Hebrew) in Haifa, a rehab centre for alcoholics and drug addicts, both Jewish and Arab. This ministry was founded by David and Karen Davis, and their vision for it has always been the "one new man" in Messiah (Ephesians 2:14–16). I've visited faith-based rehabilitation centres in the UK and abroad where the focus is purely on breaking the power of addiction. But at Beit Nitzachon they are fighting on two fronts – addiction and racial hatred – because to achieve the "one new man in Messiah" in Israel today involves demolishing the ancient wall of enmity between Jew and Arab. In today's political climate I wonder which is the greater breakthrough. David Davis told me:

> *One of my greatest joys as a pastor is to witness once lost and addicted Jewish and Arabic "sons" taking their place in the body of Messiah in Israel. Graduates of House of Victory include our youth pastor, a home group leader, a media ministry leader, as well as workers at House of Victory and Beit Yedidia, our community centre. One Arab graduate is a fearless preacher of the gospel to Muslims in Jerusalem, Bethlehem and Jericho. Only Jesus can reconcile Jews and Arabs, and He is doing it.*

Reconciliation can take time

Travel with me to Netanya, a city in Israel on the Mediterranean just north of Tel Aviv. In 1974 Lisa Loden and her husband David came from America and settled there. Former hippies, both from Jewish families, they became radical believers in Jesus and came to Israel on a one-way ticket to pursue their destiny. They were some of the first Messianic believers to come to Israel for 2,000 years. Lisa takes up the story:

"When we arrived, there was no one to greet us. Here in Netanya, the city where we chose to settle, there were no other known believers at that time."

"So what is the situation there today?" I asked.

"Today the situation is vastly different to what it was thirty-five years ago in that both the number of believers in the Messiah and the numbers of congregations have increased dramatically. When we arrived there were between 300 and 500 believers in the entire country; today, conservative estimates will tell you there are 10,000. When we came, there was no congregation in Netanya. David and I began to meet together in our home in early 1977 in faith that God would bring others and a congregation would grow here. Today the congregation, which is called Beit Asaph, numbers more than 220."

David and Lisa have always had a passion for reconciliation. I asked Lisa where that passion came from.

"I think the early experiences you have in faith affect you very deeply, and when we came to faith, we were the 'outsider' community. My husband and I came out of the 1960s wild lifestyle, so we were the outsiders in our own culture in the United States. When we came to faith we were embraced by local ordinary Christians. They loved us. They took us in. They fed us. They were so loving, and that made a tremendous impact on our lives. They didn't have to preach about unity because they lived it – they lived love. So for us it was natural and automatic that you reach out and embrace everyone."

Over the years David and Lisa have gone out of their way to meet with Arab Palestinian believers. I asked Lisa how difficult it had been.

"For me it has always been a joy. I can't say that it has been difficult. It's been painful sometimes, because when you meet people and you empathize with them and you listen to their stories and you hear their struggles and their pain, it is painful. So for me it's been a challenge at times, but always a joy to be in relationship with my Arab brothers and sisters."

The question at the heart of this book has been to find out what God is doing in Israel and the West Bank today; so why does Lisa believe reconciliation between Jew and Arab is so important to Him?

"God is a healer, and He heals hearts and He heals relationships. Our whole life in faith is about our healed relationship with our Creator, and this includes a healed relationship with His creation. How much more within the body of Messiah, which is the field of reconciliation in which I work, bringing together Jews and Arabs, Palestinians and people from the nations, in a common basis of faith and to live out in our daily lives what it means to be reconciled to God and to each other. God is doing an amazing thing here because, wherever I look, I see what I call "flowers of hope on the dusty path of life"! You look to the side and you see there's a small bloom you didn't see before. These small blooms are relationships that are being built; friendships that are formed; commitments to each other. They are small but they are truly hopeful. Some are growing larger all the time. I see it on a personal basis as well as in a number of congregations now. So God is doing something wonderful here and it's the healing of an ancient breach. I think we can look back to Jacob and Esau and Isaac and Ishmael. It's a family thing for God."

"Have you been able to do this without compromising what you believe?" I asked.

"Absolutely. I think you have to come into this area of reconciliation and relationship building, knowing who you are in Messiah – that's the most important thing. Our identity as believers in Him is the primary identity in our lives and it's on that basis that we begin to build. Then we can talk about the things that divide us. They shouldn't divide us because we do have a unity for which our Messiah died."

"So what is the atmosphere like when a group of Jewish Messianic women believers meet with a group of Palestinian Christian women?"

"Well, it depends on whether it's a first meeting, or a second meeting, or a third meeting. If it's a second or a third meeting, then there are hugs and kisses! Initially women don't come to meetings like this unless something has moved in their hearts to bring them there. Sometimes there's a bit of hesitancy, primarily from the Arab sisters because the Jewish culture and mentality is probably a little more brash and outgoing than the average Arab mentality in this country. But very quickly we get through these initial walls and we see one another as women, as people. We are all either mothers or daughters. We know that we have the same basis of faith. And even with the hesitancy there is a desire and a willingness to meet together, and quite quickly we begin to form bonds of friendship."

"You must have instances when people become angry as they remember the wrongs from the past on both sides."

"Yes, that does happen, and we've learned to keep our mouths shut and listen to one another; to put our own natural defensiveness to the side to truly try to hear one another's hearts. We cannot take collective responsibility for what our peoples have done, but we can identify with the pain that our brothers and sisters suffer and be sorry for what has happened. And we have found that it goes a long way when you reach out and touch the heart of someone else, and you lay your hand on their shoulder, or you take their hand in yours and you look into their eyes, and in that way identify with their pain. Listening and acceptance are the keys, rather than rejection of each other."

More recently Lisa has started teaching at the Nazareth Evangelical Theological Seminary (NETS), described in Chapter 14 of this book. I asked her why she was prepared to get involved in this project.

"For so long this matter of reconciliation and relationship building between our two communities has been in my heart. And this is an opportunity to actually live it out on a weekly basis. Every week I am in Nazareth and I am a Jewish woman teaching primarily Arab men. And it has been absolutely astounding! I am responsible for leadership development – spiritual leadership. It was very funny in the beginning and there was a lot of hesitation, but it was more because I was a woman than that I was Jewish. But I have to say that after the second lesson, God broke down all the barriers and we truly have a relationship of caring and love, and I have worked with them now for four years."

An unfolding story

And so the story of the Olive Tree Reconciliation Fund is unfolding. Prompted by the generosity of many Christians, the OTRF is a registered charity (number 1125706) which aims to build bridges of understanding and support in a spirit of reconciliation between believers (both Jewish and Arab) in the Holy Land (Israel and the Palestinian Areas) and Christians worldwide. I am as surprised as anybody that this has come about! It is as though we are running to keep up with what God is doing amongst His people in Israel, who cannot manage without the help of Christians in the nations. The focus of the world is on Jerusalem and what happens there, so it goes without saying how this affects the believers there.

The future?

All the projects listed above are ongoing. The OTRF is committed to supporting the people already mentioned in this book, and as news about the OTRF is spreading, understandably we are receiving more requests for help. My role is to research these requests thoroughly to be sure we are giving to genuine people.

Information

If you would like more information about the work of the OTRF please look at our website, www.olivetreefund.org and if you would like to receive regular news from the OTRF, please email enquiries@olivetreefund.org or write to the address below.

If you would like to send a gift, then please either donate online via our website or write your cheque out to The Olive Tree Reconciliation Fund and send it to OTRF, PO Box 850, Horsham, RH12 9GA, UK. If you would like your gift to go towards one particular project, please specify this.

Thank you for your generosity and interest so far. I look forward to working alongside you and keeping you informed about other people in Israel and the Palestinian Areas who need our support during the coming years in order to build bridges between us – bridges of reconciliation between Jew and Gentile.

Julia Fisher
Director of The Olive Tree Reconciliation Fund